DAVID B. PIRIE

Shelley

Open University Press
Milton Keynes · Philadelphia

Open University Press
Open University Educational Enterprises Limited
12 Cofferidge Close
Stony Stratford
Milton Keynes MK11 1BY

and

242 Cherry Street
Philadelphia, PA 19106, USA

First Published 1988

British Library Cataloguing in Publication Data

Pirie, David B., *1943–*
    Shelley. – (Open guides to literature).
    1. Poetry in English. Shelley, Percy Bysshe,
    1792–1822. Critical studies
    I. Title
    821'.7

    ISBN 0-335-15091-8
    ISBN 0-335-15082-9 Pbk

Library of Congress Cataloging-in-Publication Data

Pirie, David B.,
    Shelley / David B. Pirie.
        p.   cm. – (Open guides to literature)
    Bibliography: p.
    Includes index.
    1. Shelley, Percy Bysshe, 1792–1822 – Criticism and interpretation.
    I. Title.   II. Series.
    PR5438.P54   1988
    821'.7 – dc19   88-4255   CIP.

    ISBN 0-335-15091-8
    ISBN 0-335-15082-9 Pbk

Typeset by Rowland Phototypesetting Limited
Bury St Edmunds, Suffolk
Printed in Great Britain by Oxford University Press

Contents

Series Editor's Preface

The intention of this series is to provide short introductory books about major writers, texts, and literary concepts for students of courses in Higher Education which substantially or wholly involve the study of Literature.

The series adopts a pedagogic approach and style similar to that of Open University Material for Literature courses. *Open Guides* aim to inculcate the reading 'skills' which many introductory books in the field tend, mistakenly, to assume that the reader already possesses. They are, in this sense, 'teacherly' texts, planned and written in a manner which will develop in the reader the confidence to undertake further independent study of the topic. They are 'open' in two senses. First, they offer a three-way tutorial exchange between the writer of the *Guide*, the text or texts in question, and the reader. They invite readers to join in an exploratory discussion of texts, concentrating on their key aspects and on the main problems which readers, coming to the texts for the first time, are likely to encounter. The flow of a *Guide* 'discourse' is established by putting questions for the reader to follow up in a tentative and searching spirit, guided by the writer's comments, but not dominated by an over-arching and single-mindedly-pursued argument or evaluation, which itself requires to be 'read'.

Guides are also 'open' in a second sense. They assume that literary texts are 'plural', that there is no end to interpretation, and that it is for the reader to undertake the pleasurable task of discovering meaning and value in such texts. *Guides* seek to provide, in compact form, such relevant biographical, historical and cultural information as bears upon the reading of the text, and they point the reader to a selection of the best available critical discussions of it. They are not in themselves concerned to propose, or to counter, particular readings of the texts, but rather to put *Guide* readers in a position to do that for themselves. Experienced travellers learn to dispense with guides, and so it should be for readers of this series.

This Open Guide will be most usefully studied in conjunction with *Shelley: Selected Poems*. Edited, with an introduction and notes, by Timothy Webb, J. M. Dent and Sons, 1977; reprinted with corrections and minor revisions, 1983. **Graham Martin**

1. Introduction

While Shelley was still alive, vicious gossip led many to be more interested in the wickedness of what he had supposedly done than in either the meaning or the merits of what he had actually written. When his death was reported, there seems to have been some disappointment that it had not been caused by a divine thunderbolt, but only by a mundane accident at sea.

Yet his dying so young, just before his thirtieth birthday, led others to idealize him.

Matthew Arnold managed to encompass both attitudes. In 1886, confronted by a new biography's revelations about Shelley's love-life, Arnold was shocked into using terms like 'inhuman' and 'not entirely sane'.[1] Yet, he still recycled the opposite myth of an impractical visionary who was too good for this world:

> The Shelley of actual life is a vision of beauty and radiance, indeed, but availing nothing, effecting nothing. And in poetry, no less than in life, he is 'a beautiful and ineffectual angel, beating in the void his luminous wings in vain'.[2]

The repetition here ('availing nothing', 'effecting nothing', 'ineffectual', 'in vain') may protest too much. Like many commentators on Shelley, Arnold is far more politically conservative than the poetry he is discussing. He perhaps needs to reassure himself that such dangerously radical polemic will always flutter helplessly 'in the void' and never descend upon England in the actualities of social change.

One way to neutralize such poetry is simply to focus instead on the person who wrote it. An odd alliance of embittered scandal-mongers and sentimental myth-makers has ensured that Shelley's life is often, if inaccurately, recalled while the vast majority of his works are seldom read. Indeed, the reported business and actual brevity of the life still lead many people to underestimate the sheer volume of writing that he achieved.

However, Shelley was essentially an author; and the journey on which he drowned had been undertaken for a characteristically professional purpose. He was returning from a meeting with the publisher and author, Leigh Hunt, and with the most popular poet of the age, Lord Byron. They had been working on Shelley's proposal that the three of them should collaborate in launching a new, politically partisan, literary magazine in which henceforward each of the 'contracting parties should publish all their original compositions'.[3]

Hunt and Byron would, of course, have valued their young partner for the variety and quality of his achievement as a writer; but they must also have been impressed by its simple quantity: the number and length of works that he had produced since publishing the first of his three novels twelve years earlier. Even if all of Shelley's vast output in prose were to be ignored in favour of verse, he would still have to be seen as a prolific writer. Hutchinson's 1905 edition of *The Complete Poetical Works of . . . Shelley*, though now known to be in fact significantly incomplete, still runs to over 900 pages.

This brief guide cannot therefore hope even to mention most of Shelley's works. Moreover, it needs to make space for some discussion of the contemporary events and debates to which Shelley, as a socially committed writer, addressed himself. It must also explore a given poem or passage in sufficient detail to suggest some of the intricate skills deployed by a poet who saw his ideological message as inseparable from his literary medium.

For all these reasons, it cannot convey the vastness and the variety of Shelley's achievement. His writings, with their power to move one to myriad emotions, to mind-stretching thought, and even (as Shelley himself would perhaps have most wished) to action, can become for some readers a massive resource: one that constantly rewards further investigation. This Guide aims merely to suggest some angles of approach that may make that potentially life-long journey of exploration less difficult at the outset and more immediately intriguing.

You may already have noticed the overlapping titles that I have given to chapters 3, 4 and 5: 'Landscape and Love'; 'Love and Politics'; 'Politics and Poetry'. If these vague terms strike you as unpromisingly glib, fear not. I have interwoven them precisely to avoid making false promises. I cannot divide Shelley's poems up according to neatly distinct topics. Much of his most fruitful energy as a writer was devoted precisely to revealing the interconnectedness of experiences that lazier minds falsely separate. In Shelley's most powerfully redefining poems, the lover and the writer and the political activist belong inextricably together.

However, lest this should daunt you at the outset, I suggest that you begin by reading a few of his other poems which can, without too much misrepresentation, be distinguished according to their subject-matter.

Read first 'Goodnight' (Webb, p. 124) and 'To Night' (p. 161).

Both are, I think, clearly love-poems. Indeed they have in common the specific subject of an anticipated moment of sexual passion. Even so, their difference may suggest Shelley's extraordinary range of tone.

Then, please read 'An Exhortation' (p. 101) and lines 132–211 of 'Letter to Maria Gisborne' (pp. 110–12): both obviously about poetry and the writer's role; but again strikingly different in approach.

Finally, please compare 'Sonnet to the Republic of Benevento' (p. 123) and 'England in 1819' (p. 90). Both were inspired by specific contemporary events. Both explore the nature of politics and politicians. Yet the topic of tyranny is seen through such a broadly focused lens in the first, and a representative tyrant so precisely dissected in the second that between them – though each is no more than a sonnet – they can evoke the flexibility with which Shelley's verse defines politics.

I hope that this little selection will whet your appetite and motivate you to explore the next chapter about the events that made far greater poems possible.

2. The French Revolution and England at War

(i) Text and context

Poetry does not happen in a vacuum. A poem has not only an author but a target-audience. Both live in a particular society; and they do so whilst that society is in a specific stage of its historical development. The insistently precise title of 'England in 1819', for instance, suggests that we need to know something about the place and the time from which a poem speaks and to which it originally addressed itself.

'Come now', you may protest, 'we don't need any padding about the historical background. Even if the superficial forms of society do change, the most profound truth about human nature doesn't. And that's what great literature explores. Which is why it can go on speaking so movingly and so clearly, in any place or time, to all men and women'.

Shelley's verse seeks to expose and dismantle just these kinds of assumptions. It argues that our definitions of human nature – the ways in which we think, speak and write about people – do change; that such change can achieve massive alterations in the political system; and that these alterations can in turn create further shifts in what we take human nature to be.

Just a few decades ago, I might have written, in composing your imagined protest above, that great literature speaks 'to all men'; and left it at that. Then, the implication that the ideal – or at least the typical – reader is male might have sounded so natural as to pass unnoticed. Now, a phrasing that excluded women would not be mistaken for neutral brevity. It would be recognized as polemical rhetoric. Shelley was a pioneer on the issue of sexual politics. Within a few years of Wordsworth's complacent assertion that 'the poet is a man speaking to men',[1] Shelley was defiantly asking 'Can man be free if woman be a slave?'.[2] In this, as in so much else, Shelley knew he was out of tune with respectable opinion at the time; and accepted that his verse must be 'the trumpet of a prophecy'.[3]

In his day, the reform that gave English women the vote a full century later was still literally unthinkable. He was born into an England where, out of a population of about eight and a half million, just 11,000 men were rich enough to qualify as electors. It was difficult enough to imagine that society would ever grant the rest of its *male* citizens any political influence. In 1819, at least 60,000 and perhaps as many as 100,000 dissatisfied members of the working-class did march into Manchester for a massive, but peaceful, political rally, at St Peter's Field. Though there were many women's groups at the rally, the most radical of the reforms being demanded by the more extremist demonstrators was merely 'one *Man* one Vote'.

Yet even this seemed to the Manchester magistrates – and probably to most educated people in Shelley's England – a self-evidently impractical idea: one that flew in the face of all that was obvious about human nature. The ability to choose responsible leaders came naturally to no more than a tiny, privileged minority of human beings. The humanity of the vast majority (many of whom happened to be starving at the time as a direct result of government ineptitude) was of a different and clearly lower order. So, the

Manchester authorities sent in the cavalry with drawn swords to break up the meeting. There were many casualties, some fatal. The first to die was a four-year-old child. What became known as the Peterloo massacre is partly the subject of 'England in 1819'.

Politics, in the broadest sense, is the subject of nearly all Shelley's best verse; for he believed that men and women would never be fit to govern their society until they had learnt to free their own minds from a whole set of unconscious assumptions. His verse insists that the tyranny of such prejudice operates even in the most intimately personal moments of sexual love or the most solitary observations of wild landscape. So we need to be curious about what views of human nature competed in the England where Shelley learnt to read and where later he would look for readers of his own works. There is only space here to sketch a very few facts about that society. At the end of the Guide, you will find some suggestions for further reading on the period. In the rest of this chapter, all I can do is raise just some of the questions about context: questions which I hope you will go on asking yourself as you read the later chapters that concentrate on particular poems.

Please now read Timothy Webb's 'Introduction' (pp. xvi–xxx); and then the note-form biography that he offers on pp. vii–xii, before proceeding with the rest of this chapter.

(ii) The French Revolution

You would hardly ask an 'Outline of Shelley's Life' to begin before 1792, the year of his birth. But the events which were to dominate English thought throughout the period in which he wrote began three years earlier.

It was in July, 1789 that the ancient fortress of the Bastille had been stormed and its wretched prisoners set free. French soldiers had abandoned their oaths of loyalty to the country's supposedly magical king and their duty to God as defined by the Christian church. They had joined the oppressed people of Paris in open rebellion. They had accepted the message of those idealistic intellectuals who argued that a viciously hierarchical society could be transformed into one of justice, equality and love.

It was that attempt to alter a whole nation's definition of human nature which, twenty years later, when Shelley had to confront the bleakly conservative England of 1819, allowed him to believe in some elusive but 'glorious Phantom': an upsurge of transforming courage and energy which might, even after the brutal evidence of Peterloo, yet burst out 'to illumine' his own 'tempestuous day' ('England in 1819', lines 13–14).

The period in which Shelley had to maintain such hope was certainly a dark one for English radicalism. By then English politics, and to a large extent English poetry, was dominated by an older generation: a generation whose entrenched conservatism derived from their being able to remember and regret a time when they too had been lured into wild optimisms.

Wordsworth (born 1770), Coleridge (born 1772) and Southey (born 1774) had themselves been young men back in the early 1790s. They had welcomed the first news of Revolution in France, as had some of the most respectable people in English society, including Whig Members of Parliament like Sir Timothy Shelley, the poet's father.[4]

Wordsworth was to remember his early fervour for revolution as an excitement shared with an entire generation:

> Bliss was it in that dawn to be alive,
> But to be young was very heaven![5]

Even when the revolutionaries executed King Louis XVI in 1793, Wordsworth had stood firm in their defence. He argued that such bloodshed was a necessary weapon of the oppressed.[6] Coleridge had been able to express his anti-Royalist solidarity with the French armies as late as 1795:

> . . . we wage eternal war
> Against the tyrant horde of murderers,
> The crowned cockatrices whose foul venom
> Infects all Europe[7]

Southey, in that same year, could still write as if the progress of the French army and the advance of freedom were synonymous: 'the French everywhere victorious – the cause of Liberty everywhere gaining ground'. The one exception, Southey suggested, was England where the 'corrupt administration' of the Tory government was still in control and thus able to use its 'sword of iniquity' to murder the latest batch of English radicals who had been convicted of high treason.[8]

But such generous views of France's foreign policy and such bitter interpretations of the British government's domestic one did not last. The breaking-point for many English intellectuals came in 1798, when Switzerland, the mountain-walled symbol of republican independence, the society that was itself associated in many minds with democracy, fell to the invading French. It was then that Coleridge wrote his 'Recantation' or 'France: An Ode'. Here are some extracts from Coleridge's own summary which he published with the 1802 edition of the poem:

> The exultation of the Poet at the commencement of the French Revolution, and his unqualified abhorrence of the Alliance against the Republic.

The blasphemies and horrors during the domination of the
Terrorists . . . Switzerland, and the Poet's recantation . . .
An address to Liberty . . . conviction that those feelings and that
grand *ideal* of Freedom which the mind attains by its contemplation
of . . . Nature, and of the sublime surrounding objects . . . do not
belong to man as society, nor can possibly be gratified or realised,
under any form of human government; but belong to the individual
man . . . inflamed with the love of God in Nature.[9]

This new poetic manifesto redefines 'Liberty' so that the concept has
nothing to do with people trusting themselves and acting together
to change 'human government'. Instead it now has everything to
do with one humble 'individual' contemplating alone the sublime
superiority of 'God' and 'nature'.

Such a poem already presages the hostile climate in which
Shelley's verse would try to nurture a return to radical politics and
religious scepticism. In 1830, the aged Coleridge complacently
remarked:

Poor Shelley, it is a pity I think that I never met him. I could have done
him good . . . I should have laughed at his Atheism . . . sympathised
with him, and shown him that . . . I had been in the same state myself,
and I could have guided him through it.[10]

Southey, in 1812, did meet Shelley who was then just 19: the age
that Southey himself had been when the French revolutionaries
whom he then supported had dared to kill their King. But the
37-year-old Southey that Shelley met had now, like so many others,
abandoned his early radicalism. Indeed, he was now producing
explicitly propagandist prose in support of the Tory government.
Shelley reported with disgust that:

Southey the Poet, whose principles were pure and elevated once, is
now the champion of every abuse . . . He says 'You will think as I do
when you are as old'.[11]

Wordsworth too now congratulated himself on having matured
into a Tory. Living, like Southey, in the increasingly disaffected
North of England, he was terrified by the prospect of any political
influence being granted to the expanding populations of the industrial towns. France's potentially infectious 'Jacobinism can be frustrated', he wrote in 1818, but only 'by the existence of large estates
continued from generation to generation in particular families'.
Wordsworth put his new beliefs into energetic practice, working
diligently as official election agent for the richest landowner in the
Lake District, the Tory Lord Lonsdale.[12]

In Southern England, one of the wealthiest landowners at this
time was Sir Bysshe Shelley, the poet's grandfather.[13] He had been
given his baronetcy in 1806 for his services to what was theoretically
the opposing party of the Whigs. His powerful patron, the Duke of

Norfolk, like many Whig aristocrats, had indeed at an earlier stage
flirted with the democratic rhetoric of the French Revolution. He had
once proposed in public the toast of 'our sovereign, the people'.[14] But
he was really as arrogantly convinced as any Tory that the people
should go on trusting to him and to his class-allies to run the country.
For instance, when Timothy Shelley, the poet's father, was 'elected'
Whig M.P. for one constituency through such shameless ballot-
rigging that the result was annulled, Norfolk simply had him re-
elected for one of the other constituencies which were in his personal
gift.[15]

Such Whigs, by the time Shelley was an adult, were in the
embarrassing position of having at first welcomed the Revolution in
France. They had misinterpreted demands for 'government by the
people' as threatening no more than 'government *for* the people'
conducted, under a constitutional monarchy, by some paternalistic
élite, comfortingly like themselves. Events had proved them wrong
and vindicated the far more alarming predictions of the Tories. The
essential structures of wealth and privilege in France had indeed been
destroyed; and the infection of radicalism did seem to have crossed
the Channel to threaten England's own propertied classes.

As the ability to read increased amongst the wholly disenfran-
chised lower classes of Britain, dangerously democratic ideas gained
a mass audience. For instance, *The Rights of Man: Part 2* by Tom
Paine, who had been active in both the American and French
Revolutions, sold 200,000 copies within a year of its first publication
in 1792: almost one for every ten households in the country. The
demand continued so that, throughout Shelley's adult life, book-
sellers and publishers were being prosecuted for distributing Paine's
works.

The Tory government responded with savagely repressive
legislation, not only against freedom of speech but also against
freedom of assembly. It suspended *habeas corpus*, the law that had
traditionally protected British citizens from imprisonment without
trial. It employed a network of spies and *agents provocateurs* to
collect victims for its show trials and public executions. Nevertheless, those with wealth and power to lose still saw terrifying evidence
that what had happened in France might yet break out in England. It
had, after all, been self-proclaimed democrats who had slaughtered
their political opponents in Paris during the 'Terror'. Hence the
apparently paranoid reactions in London to the Luddite attacks of
1811–1812 or the mass demonstrations of 1818–1819.

By then the Whigs had long been struggling to disassociate
themselves from the radicalism that had convulsed France. They
knew that they would never regain power under the present system
so long as a vote for them could be regarded as a vote for the more
extreme reforms: reforms by which they themselves stood to lose

personally just as much as Tories like Wordsworth's hero, Lonsdale. The true opposition was growing in extra-parliamentary circles, amongst increasingly politicized artisans and labourers, whose demands threatened all factions of the class that had traditionally ruled Britain. So the Whigs had come to insist that the 'Whig Principle' involved 'a resistance to wild and impracticable theories, which are equally incompatible with the British constitution, and with a settled government'.[16] In doing so, they blurred the difference between their policies and those of the Tory government until the distinction was virtually invisible.

Such shiftiness had a profound effect upon Shelley as he grew up in a household of Whig aristocrats. Leigh Hunt commented shrewdly:

> To a man of genius, endowed with a metaphysical acuteness to discern truth and falsehood . . . such an origin . . . was not the very luckiest that could have happened for the purpose of keeping him within ordinary bounds. With what feelings is truth to open its eyes upon this world among . . . licensed contradictions of all sorts? Among the Christian doctrines and the worldly practises . . . among all those professed demands of what is right and noble, mixed with real inculcations of what is wrong and full of hypocrisy . . . Mr Shelley began to think at a very early age, and to think of these anomalies.[17]

Hunt perhaps exaggerates the ability of even 'a man of genius' to achieve a completely detached analysis of those 'anomalies' which have coloured his upbringing. Shelley never wholly abandoned the Whig notion that sufficient reform of society might eventually be achieved by aristocratic members of parliament improving that institution from within. Indeed, writing to Hunt himself for the first time in 1811, Shelley could introduce himself as a Whig: 'My father is in parliament, and on attaining 21 I shall, in all probability, fill his vacant seat'.[18]

Yet this represented only one side of Shelley's ambivalent stance. In 1812, he was literally aiming his views at the man in the street, devoting long hours to pacing around Dublin, pressing upon anyone he met a copy of his *Address to the Irish People*. The style of this pamphlet had been 'adapted to the lowest comprehension that can read';[19] and it is indeed rousingly blunt in its disgust at the appalling poverty imposed by the English government.

However, even here, Shelley equivocates as to whether the violence used in France can be a justifiable means to the ends of revolutionary change; and he soon abandoned his direct address to the Irish masses, focusing instead on the educated few – 'the young men at Dublin College'.[20] For this more select audience, he published an elegantly rephrased version of the *Address*, his *Proposals for an Association of Philanthropists*. Here, Shelley's patrician fear of mob violence and the dictatorship to which it could lead is far more candidly related back to the problematical example of France and the rise of Napoleon:

> It will be said, perhaps that much as principles such as these may appear marked on the outside with peace, liberty, and virtue, that their ultimate tendency is to a revolution, which, like that of France, will end in bloodshed, vice and slavery.[21]

Such things were indeed said: and one of the first to rebuke Shelley for his pamphlet was William Godwin, the novelist and philosopher, whose *Enquiry Concerning Political Justice* of 1793 had been such an inspiration to an earlier generation of English radicals.

Shelley had written to Godwin the previous year, praising him as the one 'veteran' of those more promising times who had not deserted the cause in these more recent 'years of persecution'.[22] But now, in 1812, Godwin condemned Shelley's Irish pamphleteering for its 'tendency to light again the flames of rebellion and civil war'. Shelley's plan to organize Irish radicals into a militant 'Association' flew in the face of what Godwin now claimed was the 'pervading principle' of his *Political Justice*: namely 'that association is the most ill-chosen and ill-qualified mode of endeavouring to promote the political happiness of mankind'. As for Shelley's addressing the common people directly, that risked the disaster that had overtaken France: 'You talk of awakening them, they will rise up like Cadmus' teeth, and their first act will be to destroy each other'.[23]

Godwin preferred to put his faith in a long-term process of education which could eventually be initiated and directed by an élite of intellectuals. These leaders must first prepare themselves. They needed to concentrate on their own reading and thinking and on discussion with each other. If some of them were to define their ideas in print, they should aim their books only at the select audience of their cultural peers: not at the mass-audience sought by demagogues like Tom Paine.

Yet, in his analysis of what was wrong with present society and in his hopes for what would ultimately replace it, Godwin was arguably more of an extremist than either Paine or the architects of the French Revolution. Their focus on the evils of monarchy and the glories of a democratic republic struck Godwin as mere tinkering. Even republican leaders were bound to be lured into a selfish pursuit of power; and private property, however redistributed, would continue, by its very nature, to encourage greed and competitiveness. Godwin looked to nothing less than a revolution in human nature. From this would emerge a community which no individual leaders controlled and no personal possessions divided. His egalitarian vision was, in the most positive and precise sense, anarchistic. He prophesied a society in which men and women would voluntarily act for the general good because that was the destiny to which the growth of human reason must inevitably lead.

Godwin's doctrine of a force that would necessarily, if invisibly, lead to the triumph of justice and disinterested love was to be a beacon in Shelley's verse from *Queen Mab* of 1813 through to *Prometheus Unbound* of 1818–1819. Moreover, some passages explicitly praise the contribution that Godwin's work had made to the cause of freedom back in the heady days of the 1790s. But one is a deliberate echo of the bible's 'How are the mighty fallen' ('Letter to Maria Gisborne', lines 192–201, Webb p. 111); and another uses the past tense as an essential part of its meaning:

> One voice came forth from many a mighty spirit,
>   Which was the echo of three thousand years;
> And the tumultuous world stood mute to hear it,
>   As some lone man who in a desart hears
>   The music of his home: – unwonted fears
> Fell on the pale oppressors of our race,
>   And Faith, and Custom, and low-thoughted cares,
>   Like thunder-stricken dragons, for a space
> Left the torn human heart, their food and dwelling-place.[24]

For Shelley, Godwin's voice – like the entire chorus of revolutionary optimists whose 'mighty spirit' had articulated the mood of the early 1790s – had triumphed only 'for a space'.

The Revolt of Islam, in which this passage appears, retells the history of the French Revolution as an action-packed parable that runs to nearly 5,000 lines. Yet, for all its narrative energy, the poem centres on a conundrum that threatens insoluble stasis. The glorious hope that the Revolution had represented initially, a full quarter of a century before the poem's own date of 1817, has in its very failure, created a cynicism which could last for ever.

The poem's opening lines confess Shelley's problem and then proudly announce the resolution with which he has met it:

> When the last hope of trampled France had failed
>   Like a brief dream of unremaining glory,
> From visions of despair I rose . . .

The Preface argues that 'the excesses consequent upon the French Revolution' and 'the atrocities of the demagogues' must be understood in the context of their history. The murderous violence of the young republic does not typify some timeless flaw in human nature. Instead it arose from that specific moment of historical change:

> Could they listen to the plea of reason who had groaned under the calamities of a social state [where] one man riots in luxury while another famishes for want of bread? Can he who the day before was a trampled slave suddenly become liberal-minded and forbearing?
> (Preface to *The Revolt of Islam*)

A society wholly free of viciousness can only be gradually 'produced by resolute perseverance and indefatigable hope . . . and the systematic efforts of generations of men of intellect and virtue'. Godwin's influence is clear here; but even in this conciliatory Preface designed to soothe his more nervously conservative readers, Shelley includes his own pragmatic commitment to 'systematic efforts'.

Shelley had to preserve his 'indefatigable hope' in spite of 'the panic . . . like an epidemic transport' which the bloodshed of the French Revolution had caused amongst minds that had once been liberal:

> Gloom and misanthropy have become the characteristics of the age in which we live, the solace of a disappointment that unconsciously finds relief only in the wilful exaggeration of its own despair. This influence has tainted the literature of the age with the hopelessness of the minds from which it flows . . . Our works of fiction and poetry have been overshadowed by the same infectious gloom.

The Preface may have a fairly specific target in mind here: Byron's huge popular success with the theatrically embittered protagonists of his earlier narrative poems. However, the works that Wordsworth and Coleridge were by now publishing, though superficially more cheerful than Byron's morbid melodramas, would still strike Shelley as culpably indulging in 'gloom and misanthropy'.

The conservative politics and the orthodox Christianity that both poets had come to adopt implied a sombre view of human potential. The radical voice established by their *Lyrical Ballads* (1798, 1800) had not been actually contradicted by Wordsworth's *Poems in Two Volumes* (1807). But in *The Excursion* (1814), Wordsworth expounded at length his reactionary views on society and his faith in orthodox Christianity, centring his argument around the experiences of a character, the Solitary, who had in youth been naive enough to believe in the French Revolution's hopes for humanity.

Shelley was profoundly shocked. In 1816, he wrote a sonnet, 'To Wordsworth', in which the older poet (who would not in fact die until 1850) is told that he is already dead. 'Deserting' that 'honoured poverty' in which he had once composed 'Songs consecrate to . . . liberty' and accepting pay from the Tory government, Wordsworth has committed a kind of suicide. He has left Shelley 'alone' to 'deplore' and 'mourn' his loss.

The sonnet is in fact an elegy: not for the specific work of the historical Wordsworth, but for an earlier period when to offer 'songs' of 'truth and liberty' was to feel less 'alone', less isolated from the class into which Shelley had been born. Its aim is to evoke an ideal through which all that was once best in recent poetry can be celebrated as well as mourned: to find a way of reaching back to the inspiration of a time before the failure of the French Revolution had soured the English imagination.

Shelley's most sustained and famous attempt at the genre of Elegy is 'Adonais': about the literal death of John Keats. Keats' commitment to the cause of parliamentary reform had led many of his poems to be interpreted as dedicated 'to . . . liberty' and the hostile reviewing which had supposedly hurried on Keats' death was essentially political in motivation. Nevertheless, in 'Adonais' too, Shelley is less interested in the biographical facts about one poet or the prospects for that individual reputation than in the revolutionary spirit which, in spite of its apparent demise in France, must be understood as innately indestructible.

Shelley's verse, in trying to usher in a transfiguring future, frequently has to do battle with the past. He writes belatedly to rekindle what a bigoted, older generation has tried to obliterate. You should find it useful, in approaching a surprisingly large number of Shelley's own, most aspiringly optimistic poems, to ask yourself how far their tone is achieved by an audible strain in seeking to rise above the 'visions of despair' left behind by France's 'brief dream of unremaining glory'.

In anticipation of the discussions of such poetry in later chapters, and as a relief from some of the gloomier facts that inevitably feature here, please read stanzas 39–55 of 'Adonais' (Webb, pp. 154–158), before proceeding to the next section.

(iii) War

Shelley was less than six months old when war between France and Britain was declared on February 1, 1793. By the time that long and bloody conflict finally ended on July 15 1815, he was nearly 23. Shelley thus spent not only his childhood and adolescence but also a large proportion of his adult life in a country at war: a country whose population, though increasing, was still relatively small (around 10 million at the 1811 census) but engaged in a war whose cost was massive. For instance, 20,000 British soldiers died during the brief, but disastrously bungled, Walcheren campaign of 1809 in Holland. When a journalist, Peter Finnerty, tried to expose this example of the government's lethal ineptitude, he was sentenced, under the censorship laws, to 18 months in prison.[24]

Shelley, reading of the case while still a student at Oxford, was roused to act. First, he advertised his new poem, *On the Existing State of Things*, announcing that all proceeds from the sale would be used 'to maintain in Prison, Mr Peter Finnerty, imprisoned for Libel'. Second, he wrote to Leigh Hunt, suggesting that, in a situation where the law now made 'any expression of opinion on matters of policy dangerous to individuals', it was time to unite all protest-groups into a single 'methodical society'.[25] Hunt, editor of *The Examiner*, had himself been imprisoned under the same law and recently prosecuted again, this time for an article attacking the army's barbaric punishment-system: an article whose title of 'One Thousand Lashes' had not exaggerated the kind of lunatic sentence through which a British soldier could be terrorized into obedience.

The government's repressive legislation, in an age when the printed word was the only medium available for influencing public opinion, inevitably drove writers to see their own professional rights and obligations as political issues. It also made the more impatient would-be reformers, like Shelley, feel they might have to abandon writing in favour of direct political action. So long as the government remained in control, a writer could not tell people what the war, supposedly being waged on their behalf, was costing in terms of human lives and human dignity.

The financial cost was harder to disguise from those who, through taxation, were footing the bill. In 1811, England spent as large a proportion of its gross national income on warfare as it was to do in 1915. The price was paid, however indirectly, by those least able to afford it. The new income tax on the propertied classes raised only 25 million pounds in 1815; whereas purchase taxes, on food and other items that ordinary people had to buy, extracted a full 67 million pounds. A worker, earning perhaps less than £25 in a year, was likely to spend as much as half of it on indirect taxes.[26]

For the labouring population, real wages fell as prices soared. Bread, that essential and emotive commodity, became far more expensive. With cheap grain from enemy France no longer available, a series of bad harvests in England created an exploitable shortage. The price of wheat trebled between 1792 and 1812 at a time when wages, for many workers, remained static. Around 500 riots in provincial areas broke out between 1790 and 1810 and of these roughly half were focused specifically on the availability or cost of basic food.[27]

Deaths from starvation increased as growing unemployment left some families with no income at all. Many jobs were lost to the industrial revolution's new machines, to the war-effort's demands for different kinds of goods and to the collapse of exports as France and England tried to blockade each other's ports. In Leeds, for instance, there were 1400 shearers in 1811 but, by the end of the next year, 450 of them had been made redundant. The nation, in 1812, could supposedly no longer afford its stockingers and weavers and croppers; yet, in that same year, the government was employing 250,000 fighting men in the army and had increased naval manpower from the pre-war figure of 36,000 to 114,00.[27]

Though the battles were fought abroad, the vast expenditure on militarization could be seen at home in the proliferation of new barracks. 155 were built in England between 1792 and 1815. Many were sited, not in the South to resist any invasion from France, but in the potentially rebellious towns of the Midlands and the North. By 1811, the army being used to control these was larger than the one that Wellington had taken to Spain for his campaign against the government's official enemy, France.

In that year, Shelley journeyed northwards and noted that the army was most thickly deployed where poverty and hunger were at their worst:

> I have been led into reasonings which make me *hate* more and more the existing establishment . . . I have beheld scenes of misery – The manufacturers are reduced to starvation . . . the military are gone to Nottingham – Curses light on them if they destroy one of *its* famine-wasted inhabitants.[28]

Nottingham seemed so close to open rebellion that by the beginning of 1812 it was being garrisoned by 3000 regular soldiers, quite apart from the local militia, the yeomanry and the police. As sober a witness as the reporter for *The Times* observed that the city had the 'appearance of a state of war'.

It was in 1812 that Shelley composed *Queen Mab*. The fourth canto of this long and wide-ranging protest-poem concentrates on war. It explores the links between the literal war against foreigners and the government's war-like stance towards its own people. I offer a fairly long extract below; partly because Webb's otherwise admirable selection offers you nothing from *Queen Mab* (or from any poem that Shelley wrote before 1816). However, Webb is not alone in judging most of Shelley's earliest poetry 'an unhappy mixture of Gothic melodramatics and political invective' (p. xxi). So, don't feel under pressure to admire all that you read here. Unlike the later poems that we shall be considering, these particular passages may deserve no more than one, fairly rapid, reading before you consider my comments.

You may find this poetry, which is unapologetically polemical in its encouragement of rage and grief, too raucously emotive. Yet, arguably, it is also intellectual poetry, striving to discover connection and cause. As you read the extracts below, try to decide whether the rhetorical style helps or hinders your grasp of the analytical substance. Consider too the possibility that much of the passage is *about* rhetoric: the ways in which words (and indeed other, more visual signs) create concealed political positions which the verse aims to expose and discredit. You might also wonder, granted that the extracts describe a society cruelly divided, what class of reader they anticipate.

In the full poem, this sequence comes at a point where the poet, having been forced to witness the carnage of a contemporary battle, is seen to 'shrink' in 'doubt and horror'. He fears that human beings may innately be this vicious; but his guide, Queen Mab, reassures him:

<blockquote>

... fear not;
This is no unconnected misery,
Nor stands uncaused, and irretrievable.   75
Man's evil nature, that apology
Which kings who rule, and cowards who crouch, set up
For their unnumbered crimes, sheds not the blood
Which desolates the discord-wasted land.
From kings, and priests, and statesmen, war arose,   80
Whose safety is man's deep unbettered woe,
Whose grandeur his debasement. Let the axe
Strike at the root, the poison-tree will fall;
And where its venomed exhalations spread
Ruin, and death, and woe, where millions lay   85
Quenching the serpent's famine, and their bones
Bleaching unburied in the putrid blast,
A garden shall arise, in loveliness
Surpassing fabled Eden.

                *   *   *

... Nature! – no!
Kings, priests, and statesmen, blast the human flower
Even in its tender bud; their influence darts   105
Like subtle poison through the bloodless veins
Of desolate society. The child,
E'er he can lisp his mother's sacred name,
Swells with the unnatural pride of crime, and lifts
His baby-sword even in a hero's mood.   110
This infant-arm becomes the bloodiest scourge
Of devastated earth; whilst specious names
Learnt in soft childhood's unsuspecting hour,
Serve as the sophisms with which manhood dims
Bright reason's ray, and sanctifies the sword   115
Upraised to shed a brother's innocent blood.

                *   *   *

Man is of soul and body, formed for deeds
Of high resolve, on fancy's boldest wing   155
To soar unwearied, fearlessly to turn
The keenest pangs to peacefulness, and taste
The joys which mingled sense and spirit yield.
Or he is formed for abjectness and woe,
To grovel on the dunghill of his fears,   160
To shrink at every sound, to quench the flame
Of natural love in sensualism, to know
That hour as blest when on his worthless days
The frozen hand of death shall set its seal,

</blockquote>

Yet fears the cure, though hating the disease. 165
The one is man that shall hereafter be;
The other, man as vice has made him now.

War is the statesman's game, the priest's delight,
The lawyer's jest, the hired assassin's trade,
And to those royal murderers, whose mean thrones 170
Are bought by crimes of treachery and gore,
The bread they eat, the staff on which they lean.
Guards, garbed in blood-red livery, surround
Their palaces, participate the crimes
That force defends, and from a nation's rage 175
Secure the crown, which all the curses reach
That famine, frenzy, woe and penury breathe.
These are the hired bravos who defend
The tyrant's throne – the bullies of his fear:

            *   *   *

Then grave and hoary-headed hypocrites,
Without a hope, a passion, or a love,
Who through a life of luxury and lies, 205
Have crept by flattery to the seats of power,
Support the system whence their honours flow . . .
They have three words:– well tyrants know their use,
Well pay them for the loan, with usury
Torn from a bleeding world! – God, Hell and Heaven. 210
A vengeful, pitiless, and almighty fiend,
Whose mercy is a nickname for the rage
Of tameless tygers hungering for blood.
Hell, a red gulph of everlasting fire,
Where poisonous worms prolong 215
Eternal misery to those hapless slaves
Whose life has been a penance for its crimes.
And Heaven, a meed for those who dare belie
Their human nature, quake, believe, and cringe
Before the mockeries of earthly power. 220

These tools the tyrant tempers to his work . . .
He has invented lying words and modes,
Empty and vain as his own coreless heart;
Evasive meanings, nothings of much sound,
To lure the heedless victim to the toils 235
Spread round the valley of its paradise.

                                          Queen Mab, IV

DISCUSSION

Melodramatic? Yes, of course, by some standards. But if the term
implies exaggeration like that of Gothic horror-novels, could we be
using it to protect ourselves from the actual horrors of that war? For
instance, the 'bones . . . unburied' of lines 86–7 are more likely to be

grisly fact culled from a newspaper than mere fancy from a novel: Byron visited the field of Waterloo, two years after the battle and found it still littered with human remains: a 'place of skulls'.[29]

There may be expressions here which are deliberately designed to shock; but many of them startle us, not into a wide-eyed wallowing in helpless emotion, but into constructive thought. The question that they pose is perhaps familiar and simple (what causes war?); but the various answers, asserted or implied, can seem unexpectedly demanding.

The openly repetitive rhetoric may at first seem to insist on blaming a simple triumvirate. According to line 80, 'From kings, and priests, and statesmen, war arose'; and the same three plurals in the same order are cited in line 104. But even here, in that simple choice of order, a subtler analysis is hinted. Priests are at the centre of the conspiracy. They are the pivot through which the magic of God's annointed monarchs can be used to mystify the most squalid manoeuvres of mere politicians. It was often under the laws against blasphemy that the government banned radical literature.

It is the priests, of course, whose sermons purvey the Christian doctrine of Original Sin, encouraging resignation to the evils of war as just one 'irretrievable' result of 'Man's evil nature' (l. 76). Yet this 'apology' for 'kings who rule' only succeeds because of 'cowards who crouch' (l. 77). The most apparently powerless readers must accept their own responsibility for war. The symbiotic relationship between rulers and ruled means that the remedy lies in the workers' own hands. Indeed Shelley chooses an image of simple manual labour – 'Let the axe/ Strike at the root' (ll. 82–3) – as the verse turns to its positive plea for a change that has to be precisely radical (etymologically 'radical' comes from the Latin term for a tree's roots).[30]

So, it is not just the thought here but also its expression which shifts rapidly. The archetypal Eden myth is at first dismissed as hocus-pocus, mere political propaganda to con the victims of each war into accepting it as 'unconnected . . . uncaused' (l. 75): just one more, meaningless but inevitable, result of humanity's 'irretrievable' Fall into 'evil nature'. But the central symbol in this dangerously potent myth, the tree of Forbidden Knowledge, is not censored out of Shelley's own imagery. Instead it is redefined as the 'poison-tree' which itself 'will fall', once we have learnt to 'fear not' and dared to take an axe to its roots.

The pestilent influence of the tree is described as 'venomed' (l. 841), dissolving the distinction between the original myth's opponents: God, with his supposedly everlasting prohibitions embodied in the tree and Satan, represented as the venomous serpent tempting humanity to self-destruction. The two, far from being eternal enemies, are allies in league against human freedom. The tree's poisonous 'exhalations' slaughter 'millions' to quench the blood-thirsty 'serpent's famine' (ll. 84–7). The towering divinity, who in the traditional myth is destined to win and who is now used to legitimize the role of 'kings who rule', belongs with the crawling snake supposedly doomed to endless defeat, the model for society's servile citizens: those 'cowards who crouch'. The two compose a single, intimidating system of thought. The establishment's 'fabled Eden', lost in an irrecoverable past, prevents its victims from imagining and attempting the truly paradisal society that could in future be found on earth: that very earth which war is now strewing with unburied corpses.

Imagery – the emblems by which we map our world, the symbolic pictures and miniature parables through which we learn what duties and rights we have – is here the poetry's subject-matter and not just a device of its style. Most obvious – and perhaps most relevant to Shelley as writer and to ourselves as readers – are the verbal images. Tyranny has 'invented lying words and modes . . . Evasive meanings' to entrap its victims in the nets around 'its paradise' (ll. 231–6).

The earlier lines about 'fabled Eden' have, of course, taught us to recognize 'paradise' as itself an example of just such 'lying words'; and lines 208–20 systematically expose the implications that lurk in three other words favoured by the ruling class: 'God': 'A vengeful, pitiless, and almighty fiend'; 'Hell': the fantasy of everlasting punishment used to intimidate the exploited into accepting that they must now endure a hell on earth; and 'Heaven' the promised reward of beliefs which are really a denial of 'human nature' and a blind faith in nothing but 'the mockeries of earthly power'. The indignity of such a faith is neatly pointed by the word order which precedes belief with fear and follows it with servility: 'quake, believe, and cringe' (l. 219).

But the sign-system in which we grow up embraces far more than words. This fourth Canto of *Queen Mab* begins with a misleadingly serene portrait of a nocturnal landscape with a castle:

Whose banner hangeth o'er the time-worn tower
So idly that rapt fancy deemeth it
A metaphor of peace   (ll. 13–15)

But, of course, flags, accurately decoded, mean the squalor of war. In lines 169–79, where the romanticized profession of a soldier is redefined into 'the hired assassin's trade', the uniform which his employers use to make the red-coat army seem glamorous is given new associations: the 'blood-red livery' now defines them as, not only simple killers, but also servile flunkeys.

Perhaps the most challenging example of society's non-verbal images is the toy given to the essentially *pre*-verbal child who is still too young even to 'lisp his mother's sacred name' (l. 108). Playing with the 'baby-sword', he learns to play-act the swaggering soldier and to associate self-confidence with violent aggression, acquiring what is the wholly 'unnatural pride of crime'. Where, in a saner society, words might later teach him to associate the tender protectiveness of 'Mother' with all that is 'sacred', he is destined instead to hear a language of 'specious names' and 'sophisms' which 'sanctifies the sword' of a savage, masculine ethic: a 'manhood' which verbally rationalizes what his war-toys taught him.

The ability 'to shed a brother's innocent blood' is thus not some irredeemably innate quality which he 'inherits' from the primeval Fall and the killing of Abel. It is taught, not only through the 'falsehood' of verbal signs, but also through the 'force' of the symbolic toys that are imposed upon the child, the games that it is compelled to play (ll. 107–20).

Once children's games have been exposed as deadly serious, the verse can offer a converse proposition: the earnest, old men who run the country may themselves be childish. Pompous posturing by seemingly 'grave and hoary-headed hypocrites' (l. 203) may claim that their policies derive from mature judgement; but actually they reflect only the irresponsible self-indulgence of spoilt children: pretence and frolic that happen to involve playing with human lives. Thus war, in a fairly precise sense, is exposed as 'the statesman's *game*' and 'The lawyer's *jest*' (ll. 168, 169). The king, with bodyguards who are 'bullies' (l. 179), is a playground tyrant and 'earthly power' is later dismantled appropriately into 'mockeries' (l. 220). In this nightmare of a nursery, there are no true grown-ups and authority is vested only in the silliest and nastiest children. It is through fairy-tales about Hell or Heaven or 'fabled Eden' and through the toy-shop trappings of scarlet uniforms or pretty flags, that they teach their victims to play the 'game' of some morally infantile 'statesman'.

If the attention I have been paying to details is justified and the larger patterns I have traced do exist, these lines perhaps anticipate a relatively practised readership – such as could be found only in the more privileged sections of English society at this time. However, you may think that I have concentrated disproportionately on the subtler and more coherent elements in a passage that sometimes does veer close to mere ranting. Certainly *Queen Mab*, at least in this section, does not aim to sound like a private meditation. Its oratorical style suggests more of a public speech. Its impassioned tone and its use of the kind of repetition favoured by demagogues might suggest the hustings.

Moreover, the loftier, abstract nouns are sometimes grounded in the kind of concrete terms that might be familiar to a barely educated audience. The image of man grovelling on 'the dunghill of his fears' (ll. 159–60) is one obvious example. No allusion requires knowledge beyond the bible; and that most widely known work supplies not only its mythical imagery, but also much of the syntax and diction. For instance, any farm-labourer who went to church or chapel could not be puzzled by the only polysyllable in this passage: 'The one is man that shall hereafter be;/ The other, man as vice has made him now' (ll. 166–67).

The sturdy directness of such lines offers an implicit rejection of those elegantly 'evasive meanings' (l. 234) that characterize the speech and writing of learned lawyers or genteel priests. Hostility to such sophisticated propagandists is implicit too in the sympathy for the uneducated poor who are themselves reduced to a blunter language: 'all the curses . . . That famine, frenzy, woe and penury breathe' (ll. 176–7).

However, curses which are only breathed may suggest that those who suffer most are least articulate; and that a poetry which limited itself to their vocabulary would not be fully able to explain their plight. There is a balancing-act, perhaps in places a rather precarious one, between being sufficiently sophisticated to interest an élite and yet remaining accessible to a large audience.

That large audience was potentially available. Two out of every three working men had some ability to read.[31] However, long working hours and the high price of candles limited the time that could be spent practising newly acquired reading skills. To the newest readers, deciphering each sentence was too slow a process for full comprehension of lengthy, complex arguments. Vocabulary too was often severely limited and working-class activists could make poignant misreadings of key-words in their own movement's rhetoric. Some of those who joined the Pentridge rebellion of 1817 took the call for a new 'provisional government' to mean that the hungry poor would at last have rulers who would supply enough provisions. Pitmen in 1819 interpreted 'Universal Suffrage' as unity in shared pain: 'if one member suffers, all must suffer'.[32] Of course, many labouring people were by now far more competent readers; but such examples suggest how easily Shelley might have feared that *Queen Mab* could be dangerously misunderstood by the very people that it was meant to help.

Though organization amongst the working class was growing, power to effect any immediate change still lay in other hands. And it was to that more traditional audience for literature – those whose wealth bought the privileges of education and leisure – that Shelley, with his patrician background, still often wished to appeal. But much had changed since Whig aristocrats had felt able to welcome the news of the French Revolution. By the time *Queen Mab* was being written in 1812, nearly all members of the propertied class had, for some years, been ardent supporters of the war against France. There would be little point in Queen Mab's preaching to the unconvertible; and indeed to do so might risk the book being passed on to those who would prosecute its publisher or its author.

Shelley does not seem to have thought there would be many readers who could combine the desired refinement and political influence with the necessary willingness to tolerate radical ideas. In 1813, he had Queen Mab printed in an edition limited to just 250 copies which he meant to send to named individuals. Distribution to this chosen elite went so slowly that in 1821 there were still 180 remaining copies. These were then acquired, without any authority from Shelley, by a radical bookseller. Within a few months, they had all been successfully sold amongst the largely working-class readership of a subversive journal called The Republican.

A prosecution under the censorship laws did follow. Yet, by the end of the next year, no less than four separate editions of Queen Mab were catering to the huge demand. Many other, similarly pirated editions were to appear, making the poem a significant force, not only in the early growth of English Trades Unionism during the 1820s, but also in the Chartists' struggle for democracy during the 1830s. Queen Mab also crossed both the Channel and the Atlantic to play its part in the history of continental and American radicalism.

Shelley's attitude to the early stages of Queen Mab's extraordinary popularity was highly ambivalent. In public letters to the press, he solemnly condemned the pirated edition, insisting that the it was more likely 'to injure than to serve the cause of freedom'. Yet, in his private correspondence, he claimed to be 'much . . . amused'; and wrote to more than one friend begging them to send him a copy.[33]

Some of Shelley's confusion was the deep-seated unease of the aristocratic and highly cultured intellectual wishing to speak for, but not necessarily to, a vulgarly ill-educated working class. There was also the more pragmatic consideration that the scandal over this one poem, which he had intended for a chosen few, might make other works, which he did wish to have commercially published, a target of the government and its allies in the law courts. From at least as early as 1811, Shelley had considered the possibility that his writing might land him in prison; and, when in 1812, he had left England to live in Ireland it had partly been in the hope that there he would be able to publish political poetry under his own name and yet remain free.[34]

Ireland in fact proved no safer than England; but Shelley was to end his life in exile for reasons more complex than simple fear of prosecution. The England of liberal optimisms inspired by the outbreak of the French Revolution had perished before Shelley grew up. In its place, after long years of costly war, was a nation bitterly divided into two classes. Neither of these provided an ideal audience for a poet who combined an aristocratic background with a zeal for social justice. Shelley's vision looked for an England that could be roused to transform itself, not by bloodshed leading to some new despotism, but by a wise love that would establish lasting fairness. That was easier to imagine at the distance provided by Switzerland and by Italy where Shelley would write his greatest poems.

The next chapter considers two of the earliest poems that Shelley wrote abroad. But, before you tackle these, please reconsider the propositions that I have already advanced by reading the attack on Wordsworth's recent war-mongering poetry in 'Verses Written on Receiving a Celandine in a Letter from England' (Webb, p. 7; notes: p. 193). If you have time, explore too Shelley's comic demolition of Wordsworth and his robust satire on the corruption of contemporary London in 'Peter Bell the Third' (Webb, p. 79).

3. Landscape and Love

(i) Hymn to intellectual beauty

In this chapter we will look at two of Shelley's major lyrics, both written in Switzerland. Here, in spring 1816, he had met Byron for the first time. The two poets rented houses within walking distance of each other beside Lake Geneva and spent much of the summer together. They shared the costs of a boat; and, on their most protracted voyage around the lake, called at the grim Chateau de Chillon, exploring its dungeons and torture-chambers.

They were shown round by Austrian soldiers whose garrisoning of this stronghold in once-democratic Switzerland epitomized the triumph in Europe of all that both poets loathed. Byron too despised the reactionary empires that the post-Waterloo settlement had re-established; but he liked to see himself as a realist. Chillon was yet another monument to centuries of virtually uninterrupted dictatorship and cruelty. Where, Byron could ask Shelley, was there any evidence, in the real Europe that now surrounded them, that those revolutionary hopes, articulated by the French almost thirty years ago, were ever likely to become actualities?

A more specific disagreement between the two poets was provoked by Shelley's ardent hostility to all organized religion. In the dungeons of Chillon, he would remember that many of its torturers and executioners had accepted their grisly work as a pious defence of the true faith. They had seen their victims, not as political prisoners, but as blaspheming heretics.

Byron shared Shelley's disgust at the hypocrisies of the Anglican Church in England, which was then so fervently preaching support for the Tory government. Nevertheless, he was, on the whole, far more tolerant of Christianity, and would later have his daughter brought up as a Roman Catholic. The Church's doctrine of Original Sin might be superstition; but it at least tried to explain that unhappiness which, for Byron, seemed endemic to human nature. Stupidity and greed and cruelty seemed to Byron so pervasive, through so many different societies and times, that they must have intractably profound causes. They could not be removed simply by destroying priestcraft.

Please now read Shelley's 'Hymn to Intellectual Beauty' (Webb, p. 3), considering how far it seeks to answer or to side-step these two challenges. On a first reading, you will probably find some lines puzzling; and below I will be offering some detailed advice which you can use on a slower, second reading.

However, consider first ways in which the poem may be responding to Byron's scepticism. To be specific: decide which lines, or phrases, could be quoted as evidence for each of the following propositions:

(a) The Hymn concedes that signs, in the external 'real' world, of the Power to which it trusts are rare, short-lived and enigmatic.

(b) The Hymn admits that, conversely, there are discouraging signs which are so frequent, persistent and unambiguous as to make bitter pessimism an understandable view.

(c) The Hymn is resigned to being a product of, and an address to, a culture that is still profoundly religious. It accepts the need to articulate its own faith in terms that parallel the ritual and vocabulary of Christianity.

(d) However, the Hymn explicitly denounces orthodox religion as a dangerous fraud.

(e) It dedicates itself unequivocally to a rival power, however hard the work of describing and defining that power turns out to be.

The quotations that you have assembled will have revealed many of the Hymn's themes. Nevertheless, the sequence in which the poem offers its key-statements is, of course, crucial. So I have arranged my discussion below according to the poem's own chronology. Please read again each part of the poem, deciding what it means to you, before reading the appropriate section of my comments.

DISCUSSION

The Title: (i) 'Hymn to . . .'

During the late Eighteenth Century, there had been a vast increase in the publication of Christian hymns. However, many poets had used the term 'Hymn' in the titles of works which were not religious. James Thomson (1700–1748), the hugely popular author of *The Seasons*, had indeed composed a 'Hymn to God's Power'; but he had also published a 'Hymn to Solitude'. Thomas Gray (1716–1771) produced a 'Hymn to Adversity'; and Mark Akenside (1721–1770) published both a 'Hymn to Science' and a 'Hymn to Cheerfulness'.

'Hymn' at the time thus had the potential to mean two quite different things. Shelley could be asserting belief in some divinity which exists outside of the human mind: one that is no more dependent on the poet's own moods or on his creative, verbal imagination than the Christian deity to whom Thomson prays in his 'Hymn to God's Power'. On the other hand Shelley's Hymn, like Thomson's to Solitude or Akenside's to Cheerfulness, could be invoking a mere personification: addressing itself to what is no more than a way of speaking about the writer's own, essentially human experiences and aspirations.

(ii) '. . . Intellectual Beauty'

Some critics have argued that Shelley was using the word 'intellectual' in a now outmoded sense. They translate it as 'non-material',[1] 'spiritual',[2] 'beyond the senses'[3] or 'incorporeal . . . as opposed to physical'.[4]

However, contemporary usage did already allow the word to imply the powers of the mind. For instance, Mary Wollstonecraft protests at men who patronize 'a pretty woman' by paying 'sensual homage' to her body 'as an object of desire', while ignoring her intellect:

> intellectual beauty may be overlooked, or observed with indifference, by those men who find their happiness in the gratification of their appetites.[5]

In a conventionally sexist work, some of the Hymn's phrases might suggest that the pagan deity which they invoke is essentially feminine: 'Spirit fair' (81), 'awful loveliness' (71). But Shelley, who wrote a respectful essay on male homosexuality in Ancient Greece, may have looked forward to a society in which a man too could be so described: the converse of that advance which would allow a woman to be admired as much for her brain-power, her 'intellectual beauty', as for her physical appearance. He anyway argues that what we look like largely derives from how we think. Mental energy, which this same essay calls 'intellectual loveliness', transfigures 'as with another life of overpowering grace the lineaments and gestures of every form'.[6] In the Hymn itself, 'grace' is indeed what the invoked power 'Gives' (line 36).

However, the precise phrase 'intellectual beauty' also appears in Shelley's translation of Plato's *Symposium* where the test of a powerful mind is its ability to love generously. Here, the ideal intellectual would:

> no longer . . . enslave himself to the attractions of one form, nor one subject of discipline or science, but would turn towards the wide ocean of intellectual beauty . . .[7]

This passage goes on to argue that 'the sight of the lovely and majestic forms', contained in this 'wide ocean', makes the mind feel 'strengthened and confirmed'. These 'lovely . . . forms' are to some extent those visible patterns of the ecosystem whose beauty is celebrated by landscape artists. But the point for Shelley is that we should gain confidence in the human mind, recognizing its latent power to love ever more widely, virtually creating the objects of its desire.

Indeed H. N. Cameron argues that here:

> Intellectual beauty is the beauty of the things of the mind . . . in contrast to the beauty of the external world. It is the beauty especially of the creative imagination, of poetic inspiration.

But poetry was, of course, never far from politics in Shelley's mind. The mind, at its most constructive, would build a better society. So, Cameron is surely right to add that the 'expression in poetry' of this Intellectual Beauty is:

> a power making for human progress, for it holds up a continual ideal and stimulates the mind to a creation of new objects.[8]

This imaginative power of intellect would discern the complex, but ultimately benevolent, process of history beneath the apparent stasis of Europe in 1816. Even in that dark time, the truly creative mind would occasionally catch a flickering glimpse of some future society: a mere spark of that radiant beauty which, for the time being, could scarcely be imagined.

It is possible that the entire poem constitutes an exercise in definition: a demonstration of the stance that 'Hymn' can scarcely hint; and a sustained attempt to describe that 'Intellectual Beauty' which, in the title, may be intentionally enigmatic. Certainly the title's own terms are not meant to be adequately communicative on their own. 'Beauty' alone is accepted as worth redeploying in the poem itself (line 13). For the concepts represented by 'Hymn' and 'Intellectual', the poem turns to alternative expressions.

Stanza 1

If the poem does aim to describe Intellectual Beauty, it nevertheless insists on the difficulty of such a task. The 'Power' itself remains 'unseen': only its awe-inspiring shadow can be the subject of the opening sentence; and perhaps of the whole poem.

What do you make of the *second* use, in line 2, of 'unseen'? Does this hint a daunting escalation in which even the shadow is invisible? Or do you take the idea to be that the shadow is always present among us even when our minds are too lazy to notice it?

Much clearly does depend on our attentiveness. The Power's shadowy manifestations can only be deduced from the appearance of other things through which it moves. A certain intellectual energy is required, when looking at gently waving flowers, to recognize the mild 'summer winds' that so discreetly 'creep' through them (line 4). The stealthiness of this verb – and perhaps even the fickleness in that repeated adjective, 'inconstant' (lines 3, 6) – may give fair warning that the text's own meanings must remain 'unseen', unless the reader engages them with unusual alertness and agility.

Certainly, the inverted word-order of line 5 requires some effort from the interpreting intellect. It thus compels us to experience the strenuous act of vision which is described. Please read that line again, sorting out its slippery syntax.

At first, you may have tried to understand 'moonbeams' as located somewhere behind the screen of rain falling on a pine-covered mountain: or even doubly blocked from sight, by an obscuring shower of rain as well as that tree-darkened mountain. Then, once the *syntactical* obscurity is cleared up and 'shower' is seen to be an intransitive verb, 'moonbeams' which are that verb's subject turn out to be more visible. They may, in their descent from the sky eventually disappear behind the 'piny mountain'. But, just like those falling rain-drops to which the verb so succinctly compares them, they have been in sight before the top of the mountain intervenes to hide the last stage of their trajectory.

Of course, you may think this is labouring to discover an author and his intended meaning where all that faces us is a text contorted by its own rhyme scheme: a display of verbal acrobatics that points to nothing beyond itself. But if you do accept the premises of more traditional criticism, these lines can serve as a test-case for one of its complaints about Shelley: his supposed obscurity in the choice and ordering of words. Could such obscurity, at least in this case, be acting positively: helping the reader to experience (and so to understand) the meaning which the poetry means to convey?

If so, could a comparable defence be made of the apparent indecisiveness in lines 8–11? There three quite different similes are offered in trying to catch the 'inconstant glance' with which every human being's feelings and face can be transfigured by visits from the shadow of this 'unseen Power'. The trio of alternative expressions almost playfully exhibit the very inconstancy at issue.

Consider too the sweeping inclusiveness of the fourth and final simile in lines 11–12. Could its vagueness also be appropriate, enacting the very pleasure in mysteriousness which it seeks to articulate? Or is pleasure too decisive a term for these plangent clauses. The final intensification of 'dear' to 'yet dearer' so aptly closes this lingering sentence which has run from at least as early as the beginning of line 5: a sentence which is still sighing its desire for yet more elusive beauties even as it runs out of breath.

Stanza 2

Though stanza 1 interrupts itself (notice the dashes that end five of its lines), its grammatical skeleton is essentially assertive: 'The . . . shadow . . . Floats . . . among us . . . It visits . . . Each human heart'. Stanza 2, by contrast, is interrogative. Every one of its three sentences ends in a question-mark. Are all three merely rhetorical questions? Do they just expand upon the assertions made in the opening stanza? Or do some at least introduce a new tone? If so, do they sound to you puzzled, curious, searching as if hopeful that answers can be found? Or more plaintive, more concerned to express unhappiness and to appeal for assistance?

I think the first two questions (lines 13–17), seeking an answer from the Spirit itself, *are* plaintive: though I am not sure whether we should read them as sorrowful prayers to a respected divinity; or almost bitter complaints at betrayal (such as a plaintiff in a legal case, or someone deserted by a lover, might advance).

The third question, which can be read as addressed to us rather than the Spirit, may be more rhetorical. It implicitly tells us more about the Power's inconstant visitings, adding a sombre element to the description initiated in stanza 1. There, we were asked to understand 'Intellectual Beauty' in the massively inclusive context of 'aught that for its grace may be/ Dear and yet dearer for its mystery'. Here, we must relate that power to 'aught' that tends to 'fail and fade' (line 20).

The transfiguring light of stanza 1 and the desolate gloom of stanza 2 may be equally essential attributes of this Janus-like deity whose flickering effect is both to arrive and to depart. What stanza 1 calls 'the shadow of some unseen Power' does there arrive; but as an explicitly fleeting visitor: 'visiting . . . with inconstant wing', 'it visits with inconstant glance'. What stanza 2 now calls 'a spirit of Beauty' does here depart, is indeed already 'gone' (line 15); but it is appealed to as a force whose function is to return and 'shine upon . . . human thought' like 'sunlight'.

Stanza 3

Here the poem explicitly jeers at some conventional religious terms – 'God and ghosts and Heaven'; and also perhaps the 'responses' of rituals like the Catechism. Yet it is still trying to use others positively, redirecting their emotional charge to foster reverence for an alternative deity. For instance, the associations of 'grace' (lines 36, 11) are, for a Christian reader, even more profound than line 13's 'consecrate'. Does the Hymn manage to distinguish clearly between the orthodox Christian's prayers ('Frail spells' that no voice will answer 'from some sublimer world' of a Heaven that simply does not exist) and its own plea to that supposedly active deity who '*Gives* grace'?

Shelley had written in his 'Essay on Christianity' of 1812–1815:

> We live and move and think, but we are not the creators of our own origin and existence; we are not the arbiters of every motion of our complicated nature; we are not the masters of our imaginations and moods of mental being. There is a Power by which we are surrounded, like the atmosphere in which some motionless lyre is suspended, which visits with its breath our silent chords at will. Our most imperial and stupendous qualities – those on which the majesty and the power of humanity are erected – . . . are the passive slaves of some higher and more omnipresent Power.[9]

Shelley's 'Power' is no silent absentee in 'some sublimer world'; but one that surrounds us in this one. Indeed it gives life to us as intimately, as invasively as does the air that enters our lungs.

Its manifestations are, however, like that of the wind striking a harp (the otherwise 'still instrument' of the Hymn's line 34), rare and apparently random. So, it can be praised without risk of denying the 'chance, and mutability' which is known empirically: 'we see' (lines 30–31).

Lines 32–36 offer a trio of similes (as did lines 9–11). Try to find images in the previous two stanzas that each of the new trio echoes. Line 5's 'moonbeams that . . . shower', for instance, must be recalled by line 35's 'moonlight on a . . . stream'. Are there so many such echoes that the available range of rhetoric begins to sound inadequate? If so could such self-declared deficiency be illuminating in its aptness to the poem's chosen stance and subject?

Stanza 4

The stanza begins by revising Christianity's conventional triad of Faith, Hope and Charity. Shelley, who often writes as if optimism is the highest moral duty, has no objection to the term Hope, of course. But Faith in God is replaced by '*Self*-esteem'. Some of Charity's undesirable associations are avoided by substituting 'Love'. And that term prepares the way for lines 42–3, suggesting the connection between generalized benevolence and those more specifically sexual 'sympathies,/ That wax and wane in lovers' eyes'.

Yet all three, essentially human-centred values – affection, optimism and self-respect – are not seen as originating within us. They are borrowed from outside: 'for some uncertain moments *lent*' (line 38). Can we change our own minds; or must we passively await a transformation which will be imposed from outside?

Consider the supporting ambivalence in which imagery here seems to turn itself inside out. In lines 44–5, light is equated with the internalized world of 'human thought' which is a 'flame' threatened with extinction; and darkness, which makes even the feeblest flame seem to shine brighter, represents the rescuing deity.

Admittedly, this external force has been associated with darkness before: from line 1's 'shadow', through the nocturnal references of lines 5, 9 and 35. But these last, in terms like 'moonbeams', 'starlight', 'moonlight' were arguably associated more with the light that must now stand for humanity's own inner consciousness. The latter, conversely, had in lines 21–3 been equated with darkness. There human 'fear and dream' had been the clouds whose shadows 'Cast on the daylight . . . gloom'.

Is this mobility between internal and external just an evasive shiftiness? Perhaps the equivocation is apt to an essentially transitional phase of human development. We can already imagine what a steady state of emotional sanity might feel like. Yet we are still doomed to experience much of life as *un*love, hopelessness and self-doubt. So, at least for the time being, we must rely on moods and moments whose rarity makes them *seem* alien to our nature. Those noblest emotions, though in fact our own, still feel more like the gifts of some suprahuman force: a distant power far beyond anything our own strength can yet match.

Consider lines 39–41 which may appear to suggest, not that the human heart could generate its own immortality, but that such immortality could only come as a gift from some outside force. In *Queen Mab*, Shelley imagines a reformed society which will allow each individual to enjoy a 'self-enshrined eternity'; but, in a note, he begs his readers not to 'infer that the actual space between the birth and death of a man will ever be prolonged'. Instead, since the passage of time is subjectively experienced, we have the power to expand our sense of life to what would *feel* like immortality. A society, no longer harassed by the stultifying urgencies of competition and possessiveness, would allow us to feel constantly in touch with Intellectual Beauty – or what *Queen Mab* calls 'The sense of love,/ The thirst for action, and the impassioned thought'. It is these that, for the fully awake individual, can 'Prolong . . . being':

Vivid sensation . . . makes the time seem long . . . because it renders us more acutely conscious of our ideas . . . Thus, the life of a man of virtue and talent, who should die in his thirtieth year, is, with regard to his own feelings, longer than that of a priest-ridden slave who dreams out a century of dullness. The one has perpetually cultivated his mental faculties . . . amid the lethargy of everyday business; the other can slumber over the brightest moments of his being. . .[10]

Clearly, the 'Intellectual Beauty' whose constant company would make 'the grave' less of 'a dark reality' (lines 47–8) can, at least in part, be created by the exertions of one's own intellect.

Stanza 5

The fourth stanza, as the pivotal centre of the seven-stanza sequence, has used the hopes of immortality and the fears of death to prepare the way for a more personal concern with the pattern of the poet's own life-span: from boyhood (here in stanza 5), through subsequent years (stanza 6) and finally to anticipation of his future (stanza 7).

Stanza 5 may strike you as *too* personal. Are we intruding on a private hysteria? Or are we perhaps being assaulted by self-publicising histrionics?

Neither, surely. The stanza begins by warning us that we are to hear the poet's memory of now superseded attitudes: those in which he indulged 'While yet a boy'. The adult Shelley knows that any 'uttered charm', designed to raise 'ghosts' is just as much a 'vain endeavour' as those other 'Frail spells' with which the dupes of piety try to summon the Christian God (lines 25–30). The adolescent's pursuit of the macabre took him to graveyards in 'Hopes of high talk with the departed dead'. But these hopes are delusions: comparable to those in which the youthful, still indoctrinated Shelley parroted the 'poisonous names' with which the Church of England addresses its deity.

The grown-up poet, with his insistence on courageous self-confidence, cannot be remembering nocturnal itineries designed to ensure 'fearful steps' without a wry smile. Indeed the futility of such self-indulgent melodramatics may be exposed in lines 49–54 as a carefully prepared contrast with what follows: the truly passionate moment that is recalled with pride in lines 55–60.

These initially evoke a mood that is quieter (no longer 'pursuing . . . high talk' or calling out aloud God's various names). The boy's self-conscious activities and self-assertive demands were recalled in active grammar where he was the subject governing each sentence: 'I sought . . . and sped' (line 49); 'I called' (line 53). Now, by contrast, passive grammar records the adult's more passive frame of mind: a 'me' on which the 'Shadow' can fall. The once hyperactive body seems still (patient enough to hear voices of undisturbed 'birds'). The setting too is different: more fertile and more clearly visible. Instead of the nocturnal 'ruin' hurriedly glimpsed by 'starlight', there is a presumably day-time scene where 'vital' but sleepy life-forms are seen to 'wake': at a touch as subtle and as tender as that of 'winds' that 'are wooing'.

Intellectual Beauty makes its entrance, appropriately enough, when the young Shelley's own intellect is at work ('musing deeply'); and when he is aware of the larger energies of the ecosystem, the beauties of its interactive relationships. These relationships succinctly evoke a model for the poet's own work. The 'blossoming' that intercourse with the winds produces is not an end in itself. It is the harbinger of future growth: 'News' which 'all vital things' should disseminate. If we remembered the etymological connection between propagation and propaganda, we might accept more easily Shelley's view that poetry, if it is not to be sterile, must be partisan; and, sometimes unashamedly passionate.

So, unlike the far more literal, autobiographical 'I' of lines 49–54, the first person singular who 'shrieked . . . in ecstasy' at the end of the stanza is not a self-portrait, but an archetype for all true poets. And they, Shelley argues elsewhere, are at their best no more than the humble mouth-pieces of vaster forces, working for a future that their own, individualistic intellects cannot comprehend:

> Poets are the hierophants of an unapprehended inspiration; the mirrors of the gigantic shadows which futurity casts upon the present; the words which express what they understand not; the trumpets which sing to battle and feel not what they inspire . . .[11]

Does this 'unapprehended inspiration', through which poetry grows prophetic and militant, illuminate the term 'News' which is so prominently positioned at the beginning of line 58?

Stanza 6

Consider the repeated, and ultimately emphatic, use of the second person singular here: 'thee and thine' in line 6, 'thou' in both line 68 and again in line 70 where it is reinforced by a new vocative phrase for Intellectual Beauty, 'O awful LOVELINESS'.

The poem is here perhaps most obviously a prayer. The 'clasped . . . hands', with which the previous stanza closed are a gesture – not only of intense emotion and fierce resolve – but also of supplication. The poet can claim to have prayed through many sleepless nights; for this deity accepts as appropriate homage all those activities that further the cause of liberating humanity into love. Whether the poet has been absorbed in the 'studious zeal' that produces his verse or has been practising those exercises in affection that constitute the 'delight' of making love, these moments of joy have always been linked to a prayer that the whole 'world' should be released 'from its dark slavery' (lines 64–70).

Shelley wants us to stop abasing ourselves before politicians and priests and all the false gods whom they deploy to intimidate us. He therefore has to set us an example in demonstrating, at least to some extent, that he himself has learnt 'Self-esteem' (line 37). But he has to avoid any claim to be some especially talented guru or some uniquely noble example of the generously loving mind. If he sets himself up in that way, we will either be chilled by such appalling vanity; or, worse still, the poet himself might become just another stultifying superior in comparison to whom readers learn to see themselves as pretty worthless.

Hence the device of a quite separate source of power to which even the poet must resort and to which we too can have access. It is not Shelley himself who will 'free/ This world', but that spirit of optimism and affection with which he makes contact in his best moments. He must look beyond his own, limited talents as a writer. He must hope that 'whate'er these words cannot express' will be supplied, for his readers, by that awe-inspiring 'LOVELINESS'. This word is perhaps capitalized so that we linger to read into it both the lovable beauty that even the present world does some-times offer us, *and* our own creative capacity to love it and each other.

All of us, in our best moments of 'studious zeal' or 'love's delight' exercise – and thus expand – the power to transform ourselves and the world. This does not involve any megalomaniac fantasy of single-handedly managing to 'free/ This world from its dark slavery'. Nor does it suggest the more innocent delusion that, while happily absorbed in work or love-making, one can be selfless enough to ponder all that needs to be done for an enslaved society. But, Shelley implies, the right *kinds* of work and love-making will automatically nudge us towards a more selfless attitude. They grant the sort of 'joy' by which we are a little more 'illumined'. By their light, we can recognise the wastefulness of a 'dark slavery' that runs deeper than any specific social reality (such as the literal slave-trade which was still thriving in Shelley's day). We must also set 'free' our own 'heart[s]', dethroning those more subjective, less obviously political forces of fear and bitterness which 'Keep . . . state' where Intellectual Beauty alone should reign (lines 39–41).

Stanza 7
Do you think the imagery in lines 73–7, though still referring to the natural world, strikes a different note from the first three stanzas' fleeting – and arguably subjective – moments of vision?

Stanza 1's 'moonbeams' can only be partially glimpsed before they vanish 'behind some piny mountain'; and, if we read with extreme precision, Stanza 3's 'moonlight on a *midnight* stream' is a beauty visible for but one second. They typify those alterations of light upon landscape which 'depart and come' at innately 'uncertain moments': ones that can never be anticipated (lines 37–8).

Moreover, neither is a literal sight. Both are mere similes. In the opening stanzas, what the poet perhaps *has* sometimes seen is used merely for comparison: to evoke (and *in*voke) what must itself remain '*un*seen' (lines 1 and 2).

Surely, lines 73–6, with their confident grammar of assertion, are strikingly different, replacing the 'inconstant glance' with a steady gaze that can report certainties. The day's gradual shift, once feverish noon is over, into the gentleness of a 'more solemn and serene' light *is* predictable: at least in the reliable climate of Switzerland in summer; and, anywhere in Europe, summer will be followed by autumn.

Yet the annual cycle of the seasons is long enough to allow one often to forget what a given time of year actually feels like. In the midst of some dazzlingly hot, apparently endless summer, any change can be almost unimaginable. The subtler 'harmony' of autumn and the utterly different 'lustre in *its* sky' can seem impossible: 'As if it could not be, as if it had not been' (lines 74–6). After all, throughout such a summer, no evidence of such a future can be either 'heard or seen' (line 76). But a determined empiricist like Byron (even at blazing noon on the hottest day of that argumentative summer of 1816) would have to concede that autumn – with all its extraordinary transformations – would eventually arrive.

Notice that, for Shelley, the arrival of autumn is equated with the movement from morning to afternoon: not with the later, chillier movement from afternoon to evening. Wordsworth's famous 'Immortality Ode' (published 1807) had focused its resignation to the advancing years on dusk:

> The clouds that gather round the setting sun
> Do take a sober colouring from an eye
> That hath kept watch o'er man's mortality.   (lines 197–9)

Shelley welcomes the future as a warming afternoon promised by 'onward life'. The 'Immortality Ode's prediction of inevitable decline – 'shades of the prison-house begin to close/ Upon the growing boy' (lines 67–8) – is directly answered by the Hymn's insistence on growth as progress: from boyish self-indulgence interrupted by a moment of inspiration (stanza 5), through dedication and a faith maintained (stanza 6), towards an ultimate liberty.

This liberty depends on abandoning timorous respect for external deities. The word 'fear', in the last line, is used in its traditional, biblical sense of reverence; but what the poet here respects so fearsomely is not God. Instead, he has learnt 'to fear himself'; and, through that discovery of his own exemplary value, he has come to 'love all human kind'. In the end, the Hymn invites us to see further than that 'awful shadow' of an 'unseen Power' with which it began, by looking closer to home. There, we might discover an intellectual and emotional strength that is – not merely, but formidably – 'human'. Together, we ourselves constitute the most awe-inspiring force in the universe.

The best gloss, not only on the Hymn's closing line, but perhaps on its entire prayer to Intellectual Beauty, may be this passage from Shelley's 'Essay on Christianity':

> ... were ignorance and envy and superstition banished from the world, all mankind would be as friends. The only perfect republic is that which comprehends every living being ... You ought to love all mankind, nay, every individual of mankind; you ought not to love the individuals of your domestic circle less, but to love those who exist beyond it, more. Once make the feelings of confidence and affection universal and the distinctions of property and power will vanish.[12]

The passage concludes that only through such 'confidence and affection' can we disperse 'the gloom of tyranny and slavery – ministers of mutual suspicion': a process obviously similar to the Hymn's faith that 'self-esteem' and 'love' can 'free' us from 'dark slavery'.

Yet the Hymn may be as much about poetic inspiration as social change. 'Intellectual Beauty' may be partly what other poems call the Muse. So, consider the relevance of another passage of Shelley's prose:

> Poetry is the record of the best and happiest moments of the happiest and best minds. We are aware of evanescent visitations of thought and feeling, sometimes associated with place or person, sometimes regarding our own mind alone, and always arising unforeseen and departing unbidden, but elevating and delightful beyond all expression ... It is as it were the interpenetration of a diviner nature through our own; but its footsteps are like those of a wind over a sea, which the coming calm erases and whose traces remain only as on the wrinkled sand which paves it.[13]

If the hymn is to some extent about poetry, and if the moods that inspire verse are indeed 'beyond all expression', then the poem may often – and not just in the one line gesturing to all that 'these words cannot express' (line 72) – evoke its own inadequacy; and perhaps the inadequacy, for the present, of all poetry.

However, the poem explicitly values and pursues confidence: not only the larger 'hope' that some stable, and universally shared happiness does await future generations; but also a more specific 'self-esteem': a faith in the contribution that 'these words', for all the limitations of the present, can make to the achievement of that future. How would you weight these alternative emphases?

For me, some of the hymn's plaintive rhythms and forlornly
tentative syntax do evoke an almost despairing self-doubt. It seems a
poem which struggles through the net of its own exquisite poign-
ancies, fumbling for a freedom that at first eludes it. However,
the poem arguably aims to demonstrate, and not merely to describe,
the difficulty of its own project. If the tough-minded serenity which
its final stanza achieves had not been so audibly earned, could its
closing lines sound so convinced and convincing?

To find your own way of answering that question – and others
that I have raised about Shelley's views of the natural world, human
love and the role of poetry itself – please read three other poems
before proceeding to the next section. First, read 'Song' (Webb, p.
102) whose opening lines – 'Rarely, rarely, comest thou,/ Spirit of
delight' – announce its stance as obviously comparable to that of the
Hymn. Then, read 'To a Sky-lark' (Webb, p. 104). Finally move to
'The Cloud' (Webb, p. 98) which you may find more of a contrast
since here aspiration has already become achievement before the
opening line. This poem's own voice speaks for – not to – those
liberatingly fluid, eternally creative forces that the other poems
merely invoke: 'I change, but I cannot die' (line 76).

(ii) Mont Blanc

Shelley wrote this poem after a trip which had taken him from the
lush pasturelands around Lake Geneva to Chamonix, the village that
is perched amongst Europe's highest mountains. One of the ways
in which the Hymn and 'Mont Blanc' may form a matching pair is
that they respond to two quite different kinds of landscape which
contemporary readers might have called the 'beautiful' and the
'sublime'.

According to Edmund Burke's *A Philosophical Enquiry into the
Origin of our Ideas of the Sublime and Beautiful* (1756), the 'Beauty'
in the small-scale features of easily accessible kinds of countryside
'excites in the soul that feeling which is called love'; whereas 'the
passion caused by the great and sublime in nature', such as the Alpine
peaks, 'is Astonishment . . . with some degree of horror'; or even
'ideas of pain and danger'.[14]

'Mont Blanc', in spite of its own apparently localized title and
sub-title ('Written in the vale of Chamouni'), may be far less interested in describing a particular landscape than in using it to
explore 'the origin of our ideas'. But how far is it interested in our
aesthetic assumptions about natural beauty? Is its restless enquiry
more concerned with the basic issue of whether our minds create all
that we seem to observe; and if so, whether we read into landscape,
however unconsciously, value-systems which are innately political?

Please read the poem now, keeping these questions in mind.

DISCUSSION

'Mont Blanc' is a difficult poem, not least because the poet sometimes represents himself as baffled. In lines 34–40, his contortions, as he struggles to observe the workings of his own mind, produce a 'dizzy' vision, a 'trance' at least as 'strange' as it is 'sublime'. In line 57 his mind explicitly 'fails' to make sense of the bewildering landscape. The interrogative grammar of lines 71–4 is resorted to again in the very last lines so that even these are still posing questions that the poem itself cannot answer.

The mountain, apparently announced in the title as the poem's subject, proves elusive. It does not appear until line 61 and then only briefly, not reappearing until line 127 which is almost an apology for the fact that 'Mont Blanc', still awaiting adequate verbalization, 'yet gleams on high'.

Indeed, is the poem ever committed to persuading us of some real locality that could exist beyond its own margins? Its verbal gestures in such a direction often seem to elide the literary sign-post and any supposedly literal destination. Section I may be about a river, and the terrain through which it flows; but both are metaphorical. Challengingly enough, amongst the myriad things which the metaphorical river represents are what we might normally call real rivers; for it symbolises the entire 'universe' of visible 'things': all that concrete imagery which 'Flows through the mind'. Yet, in the poem's own imagery, neither this current (which contains only our own impressions of rivers); nor its valley (which represents, not a material skull or the physiology of brain-cells, but the mind itself) have any concrete existence.

Admittedly, in the first line of Section II, the literal valley leading down from Chamonix is announced, under its proper name: the 'Ravine of Arve'. But it is invoked only after a 'Thus' which invites us to see this ravine as interesting, not in itself, but because its function is comparable to the human mind through which the 'universe of things/ Flows'. Similarly the specific river that actually does flow down from the glaciers of Mont Blanc, through Chamonix, along the ravine and on into the Rhine, is introduced by name at line 16. But its first use here is as a mere simile for what interests the poem more: 'Power'. It is this which *'in likeness* of the Arve comes down/ From the ice-gulphs that gird his secret throne'.

The male and monarchical denotations of 'his ... throne' personify the mountain as a king. Most European minds, when the poem was written, one year after Waterloo, were resignedly royalist. What then seemed a natural view of Nature's power entailed reverence for Europe's highest mountain as an imperial king of kings, surrounded by its 'subject mountains' (line 62). Mont Blanc earned that name because its height, even in the hottest summers, ensures that it remains unvaryingly white with snow. So it might seem innately well-equipped to symbolize the propriety of undeviating stasis. Its apparently unalterable shape bulks so large as to look like some ultimate proof of conservative faiths: that God created the earth according to a design whose larger outlines never vary; that certain divinely appointed kings and priests are such spectacular peaks of human excellence that they inevitably inspire awe; that the mental habits of humbling ourselves are as immutable as the laws of nature which keep the valley so far below the mountain.

Shelley's poem announces that Mont Blanc can eventually be seen in terms that will 'repeal' such 'codes of fraud and woe' (lines 80–1). However, the poem does not exclude traditional, implicitly conservative ways of describing landscape. It recycles them to serve an opposite cause.

Thus, Sections I and II do include words like 'everlasting' (line 1), 'forever' (line 9), 'ceaselessly' (line 11), 'ever' (line 22), or 'eternity' (line 29). But, here, these terms do not reverence the stasis of some supposedly objective landscape: one which God created and which it is our humble role merely to observe. Instead, these terms focus on 'ceaseless *motion*' (line 32). They celebrate that 'unremitting' energy with which the 'human mind' shapes and changes the universe which it experiences (lines 37–40).

One of the poem's most crucial strategies is to begin, not with the stable mountain, but with a fluid river and one whose dynamism is determined by our own intellects. Any seemingly stationary and external landscape in fact 'Flows' through 'the mind'. Just as the breadth and depth of a river is moulded by the valley through which it must move, broken into deafening turbulence at one point and smoothed wide into gently moving pools at another; so things move through a human mind which has the power to shape all that it contains.

But, perhaps this is to overstate. The flexible punctuation and appropriately fluid syntax of Section I (all of whose 11 lines form a single sentence) allow various readings. There may be *two* watercourses here. If so, the poem may equivocate as to which has the greater power. So, please read Section I carefully again.

DISCUSSION

The river that 'Flows . . . and rolls its rapid waves' in lines 1–4 may still be what is being described in lines 3–6 as 'The source of human thought', that brings 'its tribute . . . waters' from 'secret springs' (lines 3–6). In line 5, we can apply 'its' all the way back to the 'universe of things' and see that as the junior potentate having to pay 'its tribute' to the superior, human 'mind'. The mind, on this reading, is represented throughout Section I, not as a water-course but as a valley; and as the extensive landscape beyond ('woods . . . mountains', line 8); and even as the climate ('winds', line 10). Through these, the river of mere 'things' is channelled; and from these it derives its significance.

Alternatively, the 'secret springs' of line 4 may point to the modest origins of a quite different stream: one 'of human thought'. It would be this, newly introduced stream which would be paying 'its tribute' in line 5, the 'its' referring back no further than this second stream's 'source' at the beginning of the same line. The stream of human consciousness might be a mere tributary to the river of 'things'.

It matters because we are about to meet, in line 7, what on its own would remain no more than a 'feeble brook' and which is indebted for half the noise it makes to something else. If this still refers to the same river of 'things' that 'rolls its rapid waves' through lines 1–2, then it is the earth that would be relatively weak and inarticulate on its own; and that can only be turned into the 'vast river', which 'bursts and raves' in lines 10–11, through the human mind. However, we may take the 'feeble brook' to refer back to a separate stream introduced in lines 5–6, one coming 'from secret springs' that are 'human thought'. Then, it would be our own intellects that are relatively weak until augmented by 'The everlasting universe of things'.

Perhaps Section I's ambiguities do allow for that self-doubt which tempts us to see the physical earth's pre-existing forms as more potent than our babbling minds. Yet we are surely invited to seize the opportunity of a bolder interpretation. Perhaps it is we who can transform the bland little brook of sense-impressions by channelling it through a mental landscape of aspiring energy and turbulent struggle:

> Where waterfalls around it leap for ever,
> Where woods and winds contend, and a vast river
> Over its rocks ceaselesly bursts and raves.   (lines 9–10)

You may think that 'waterfalls' (unlike 'woods and winds') belong to a river rather than to its surroundings. But are they not created by the rocky terrain down which they are compelled to plunge? And they may reflect the weather raging over the wider scene where 'woods and winds *contend*'. A violent storm can swell what has for ages been no more than 'a feeble brook' until it 'bursts and raves' far beyond the confines of its traditional banks.

Moreover, a human observer can to some extent choose what pattern to impose on the anarchic mass of impressions that a wide landscape offers to eye and ear. We can decide just 'Where' we will locate the central significance of such a scene. We can choose the feature that should be identified as the source of its power: just as we can interpret waterfalls as the products of either river or rock. So, it is the climate of our own ideas and the topography of our own images which make the natural world into an example of resigned trickling or defiant flood.

Certainly, Section II takes as its starting-point, not the river itself, but the shaping 'Ravine' through which it must flow, the 'vale' whose 'many-coloured, many-voiced' influences determine its shifting, multifarious appearance and implications. The alternation of 'Fast cloud-shadows and sunbeams' (line 15) suggests that the Arve too 'Flows' as a volatile, subjective construct, 'now glittering – now reflecting gloom' (line 3). Our fluctuating definitions of the external world may be optimistically self-confident or gloomily servile, depending on just what we take the ultimate power to be and on precisely where we imagine it residing.

Long-established habits of thought compel us to see the massive mountain of Mont Blanc as embodying *some* sort of power. All too easily, the massive outlines of its present shape can be seen as having existed unaltered since some primal moment of Creation. If its ascendency far above more lowly terrain is thought of as God's original dispensation, it can seem to sanction those traditional political systems where kings claim divine right; and hierarchy is regarded as an immutable, natural law. For Coleridge, writing his 'Hymn . . . in the Vale of Chamouni' just seven years earlier, Mont Blanc epitomized the naturalness of inequality and the benevolence of the God who had ordained it. Coleridge tells the mountain that its job, as one supreme ruler co-ordinating reverence for another, is to articulate the need for respect:

> Great Hierarch! tell thou the silent sky,
>   And tell the stars, and tell you rising sun
>   Earth, with her thousand voices, praises God.

Here the myriad voices of earthly things are all reduced to chanting but one interpretation of their role.

'Mont Blanc', by contrast, relies on the versatility of a human consciousness that is limitlessly '*many*-voiced' in its own power: the power to *re*interpret. Shelley – who chose to describe himself in a Chamonix hotel register as spokesperson for Democracy, Philanthropy and Atheism – trusts that the mountain can itself be given 'a voice . . . to repeal' those very 'codes of fraud and woe' which Coleridge had made it articulate (lines 80–1).

Please now read again Sections II and IV, trying to distinguish at least two ways in which the mountain, with its glaciers, is made into a more subversive symbol.

DISCUSSION

On the one hand, since this 'Power dwells apart . . . Remote . . . and inaccessible' (line 97), rulers who identify their cause with such mountainous authority can be seen as unintentionally revealing their utter indifference to the suffering of their subjects. In spite of their claim to represent on earth the power of an essentially benevolent creator, they are as savagely inhumane as this 'Ghastly, and scarred, and riven' snowscape where eagle and wolf scrap over human bones (lines 68–9). In lines 104–20, the icy architecture of the privileged ('dome, pyramid, and pinnacle . . . tower/ And wall') is a 'city of death': 'impregnable' in its disregard of ordinary people and the things which they cherish.

On the other hand, the superficially immobile mountain can be seen dissolving into its fluent glaciers. And these literally rewrite the map: destroying a forest here, building 'many a precipice' there. Mont Blanc can thus be described in terms which evoke the inevitability of change: the melting of all present forms of order into the 'rushing torrents' of some new, irresistible force which, one day, will be 'The breath and blood of distant lands' (line 124). The text thus moulds the mountain not only into a 'hideously . . . rude' articulation of present rigidity (lines 69–70); but also into an exhilarating promise of future fluency.

You may think that these two reinterpretations make uncomfortable bedfellows. If we are to see the melting mountain both as a dictatorial monarchy *and* as the coming revolution, may we not fear the latter as a force to which almost as 'much of life and joy' may be 'lost' (line 117) as is now being sacrificed to current regimes? If the revolution's own momentum is to be just as glacier-like, how many human beings will suffer as much for this new cause and see their 'work and dwelling/ Vanish, like smoke before the tempest's stream' (lines 117–20)? Do you think the reader can commute, without confusion, between Mont Blanc as an image negatively exposing callous destructiveness and the use of its glaciers as symbols that positively reveal the life-giving irrigation that will energize 'distant lands'?

Of course, the price of revolution may only need to be paid during a given historical moment, beyond which, however 'distant', may lie a Utopia in which all violence has become unthinkable. But, with the horrors of the French Revolution such a recent memory, Shelley may be consciously struggling with a pair of reinterpretations that threaten to become mutually exclusive. He does so, however, in an imagery which invites us to believe in apparent irreconcilables: we all know that ice and water are – and yet are not – the same; that the permafrost on Mont Blanc's peak is connected by indisputable links to the lush crops growing beside the Rhine.

The poem is anyway candid about posing questions to which, at least for the time being, 'None can reply' (line 75). And in spite of the two new voices that the poem struggles to supply, Mont Blanc is still to some extent preserved as an 'inaccessible' enigma. In the fifth and final section of the poem, repetition stresses that the mountain functions 'silently'. It 'broods' in a pregnantly 'secret strength' which 'none beholds', nourishing a destiny which cannot yet be envisaged. The poem's last sign is a question-mark. Just before that, its last word – 'vacancy' – seems almost to anticipate the blank uninformativeness of the white, unmarked paper to which the print of this text then gives way.

Is this just a maddening refusal to deliver the goods? More specifically, what can the value of 'vacancy' be as conclusion to a poem which has earlier been so busily filling in this oppressively blank landscape with fresh implications? Is there any way that this reduction of the mountain until it is virtually 'voiceless' (line 137) can seem consistent with the earlier attempts to *give* it 'a voice': one potent enough 'to repeal' entire 'Codes' of language and thought (lines 80–1)? Please read Section V again now.

DISCUSSION

Shelley also uses this term 'vacancy', at a point in his 'Essay on Life' where he has just been advancing what is clearly one of the poem's own premises: 'that nothing exists except as it is perceived'. The value of this view, according to the essay, is precisely that:

> It establishes no new truth . . . It leaves, what is too often the duty of the reformer in political and ethical questions to leave, a vacancy. It reduces the mind to that freedom in which it would have acted but for the misuse of words and signs, the instruments of its own creation.[15]

Even the most resolutely radical writer cannot escape infection from the particular 'misuse of words and signs' which is integral to contemporary language and culture. But some sort of reaching back to the clean slate of non-verbalized experience may be possible: a recovered 'freedom' of silence out of which some better use of words and symbolic signs could eventually emerge. If the '*mis*use' built into current usage must risk yet again persuading us to accept present convention as unalterable truth, a liberating poem must not articulate some 'new truth' as instant replacement for the old one. It will not bully us, as fast as we reject the king's authority, into accepting the poet's.

The patterns of future thought, the forms of future society are to be shaped later by a free people who will be so transformed that their wishes cannot be anticipated. For the time being, the intellectual's task is perhaps merely to dismantle some of the mental limits within which we have to operate: to create a space in which we can make up our own minds.

However, the concept of vacancy is also deployed in the 'Hymn to Intellectual Beauty'. There, by contrast, it is an unequivocally negative force: a world that is left 'vacant' is 'desolate' – a 'dim vast vale of tears' ('Hymn', line 17). Apply that to the rhetorical question in which 'Mont Blanc' closes and you get a very different reading. Perhaps here too we should interpret 'vacancy' not as a latently fertile womb but as a sterile vacuum. Then the poem ends by putting the mountain in its place as a phenomenon that depends, for its very existence, on the creativity of human thought.

However, remembering the balanced 'interchange' which both 'renders and receives' (lines 35–40), we could see this, not as a one-sided jeer, but as an implicit celebration of partnership between the 'universe of things' and the vision of our intellects: the earth needs the 'human mind's imaginings' if its grandeurs are to be appreciated; but we have an equal need of those visible grandeurs if we are not to be literally empty-headed.

You may find it useful to compare the closing lines of both 'To a Skylark' (where what the poet hears he cannot make audible to the world) and 'The Cloud' (whose celebration of creativity ends with an act of wilful *de*construction).

In this chapter, I have tried to display Shelley's complexity of thought and subtlety of expression by tackling, in considerable detail, just two of his major lyrics. Both poems were written at much the same time; and both explore the relationship between the human intellect and the earth that it contemplates or creates. Yet they are surely very different; and, even within each poem, the variety of approach requires us to see the interconnectedness of ideas that we tend to keep separate. For Shelley, images of the so-called 'natural' world are dependent on the view that we take of our own, and each other's, essentially human abilities. The yearning, both for 'self-esteem' and for the courage to care about our fellows as equals, makes landscape inseparable from our latent power to love.

For a darker view of the relationship between the earth and even the most charismatic of human minds, please read 'Lines Written on Hearing the News of the Death of Napoleon' (Webb, pp. 41–2). Here Earth describes herself as having been 'a 'sullen ... frozen chaos' until she grew warm under the pressure of 'Napoleon's fierce spirit' and melted into 'A torrent of ruin'. The comparison should help you to judge what 'Mont Blanc' (or indeed the 'Hymn') gains and loses by being so much less explicit about its origin in the specifics of recent history. You might particularly look at the last two lines of the Napoleon poem. These spell out more bluntly that difficult balancing-act – between 'shame' at our present lot and proud 'hopes' for our future – which 'Mont Blanc', like so many other Shelley poems, must attempt.

4. Love and Politics

We turn now to some poems in which the intertwined themes of 'love' and 'politics' emerge, not from the scenery of the natural world, but from some situation that is more obviously human: a meeting of old friends in 'Julian and Maddalo', the poet's desire for an idealized woman in 'Epipsychidion', and the statue of a dead king in 'Ozymandias'. More briefly, we shall also be looking at four of Shelley's shorter lyrics.

'Julian and Maddalo' originated in an actual meeting between Shelley and Byron at Venice in 1818, the first since their summer in Switzerland. They again took up those arguments of 1816 which had helped to inspire 'Hymn to Intellectual Beauty' and 'Mont Blanc'.

If 'Mont Blanc' can only be approached with a mountain-climber's nerve and patience, 'Julian and Maddalo' is one of Shelley's more relaxingly accessible poems. Its seaside setting seems apt to a work whose opening tone is leisurely, intimate, almost conversational.

Since Maddalo is as much a portrait of the real Byron as Julian is a *self*-portrait, Shelley's poem flatters his companion's taste for earlier, Augustan poets by using their favourite verse-form of the heroic couplet. The cool rationality with which that form is often associated perhaps risks giving too much of an advantage to one side of the debate. Maddalo and Julian are, of course, differently de-scribed but since both must speak within this same couplet form throughout, there is perhaps a risk of Julian sounding as resignedly cool-headed as his opponent.

Yet you may decide that Shelley's use of the couplet in fact proves so flexible as to raise a quite different problem. The poem may embrace such a range of tones as to risk fragmentation. Both as debate and as narrative, it flirts with the options of moving in various directions. Its style, which at first sounds almost prosaically casual, later expands to include strident expressions of anger and misery. On a first reading, you may wonder just how seriously you are meant to play this literary game – or set of games; and you may still feel puzzled – and perhaps momentarily disappointed – as you read its last line.

To enjoy it as an intriguing conundrum, try to notice where and how it alters its tone. Consider, too, whether the overall, narrative voice is identical with Julian's: do you sense any ironical distance between what the text presents of Julian and the character's own view of himself? The Preface, after all, concedes that 'Julian *is* rather serious' (Webb, p. 13).

However, your priority on a first reading should be to identify the different attitudes adopted by Julian and Maddalo. Please read the poem now (p. 12).

DISCUSSION

At first, Julian is shocked by the fate of whole generations who have accepted from 'age to age' the 'uses vile' of the prison (line 100). Its bell summons the inmates to some superstitious ritual which suggests that their misery is God-ordained: a 'dark lot' imposed, not by their own servility or the viciousness of those more privileged, but by some 'stern maker'. Their being manipulated into feeling some 'need to pray/ In thanks or hope' to such a callous creator seems grotesque, illogical. So too does the idea that supposedly mindless lunatics have the intellectual 'skill' to understand any of the pious phrases that they are made to chant (lines 111–13). Julian sees 'religions and old saws' as harmful because they teach that humanity is by nature weak.

His is 'another faith'. As adults we have 'subjected' ourselves to 'sick thoughts'. We have allowed ourselves to be imprisoned by conventions of despair which are in fact quite alien to us. Our true, original, 'teachless nature', still visible in the child, is essentially optimistic and libertarian: 'blithe, innocent and free' (lines 159–70).

Maddalo's values are less politicized, more personal. His sense of pathos is stimulated by a mortality that dooms each individual mind to extinction. The madhouse and the institutionalized religion that it represents are acceptable to his genteel pessimism. Innate and unalterable deficiencies in human life make such architecture apt enough. Indeed, the building can even be enjoyed aesthetically. What offends Julian as a 'deformed and dreary pile' (line 101) appeals to Maddalo's gloomy sensibilities as a 'heaven-illumined tower', lit by the poignant beauties of the fading sun (lines 124–30).

But, as narrator, Julian too sometimes sounds close to this way of seeing. At one point in his description, 'churches . . . and palaces' have no distinct significance as ecclesiastical and aristocratic power-bases. Instead, they merge with 'The orange hues of heaven', sinking 'into the purple sea . . . silently'; and that silence infects Julian's voice of protest as much as Maddalo's rhetoric of resignation: '*We* hardly spoke' (lines 132–40).

Julian as character sometimes moves close to Maddalo's calm resignation. But, as narrator, he is compelled to record that the Madman's speech is 'all the while' accompanied by 'the loud and gusty storm' which 'Hissed through the window' (lines 295–6). The reader can remain interested in that storm-challenged building and not focus exclusively on the one inmate whom the friends are visiting, and to whom Julian arguably over-reacts. Remember his confession: 'I never was impressed so much'; and that arguably obsessive 'zeal' for but one member of a suffering race (lines 517, 564–81). At the end, we may choose to recall what Julian perhaps increasingly forgets: the larger insights that earlier in the poem he himself offers.

Please now reconsider the initial dialogue of the two friends (as summarized and quoted in lines 28–132) and compare it with their two conversations the following day (lines 159–270 and 534–46). Remember that between these last two passages we hear the Madman's own voice. Is it that intervention which allows Julian and Maddalo, however momentarily, to sound more at one with each other: ('we agreed . . .', line 525)?

Notice also that the first of these two dialogues is immediately preceded by a portrait of Maddalo's daughter (lines 143–58); and that the second is soon followed by the description of her as a grown-up: with that tantalizing extract from her own remarks about the Madman (lines 588–617). The trivial games 'played' by her as a child (line 143) give Julian the basis for his famous assertion of human dignity and intellectual power (lines 167–77). Please look at that again, noticing other ways in which it may be modified or supported by the overall context of the entire poem. And consider some details. How, for instance, is our understanding of Julian's 'enchains' or 'chains' (lines 171, 181) affected by the literal 'chains' in line 181; or by the rather different, more self-absorbed 'chain' metaphorically deployed by the Madman in line 302?

How do the interventions of the Madman and of Maddalo's daughter complicate our understanding of Julian and of Maddalo?

DISCUSSION

Both Madman and daughter compel Julian and Maddalo to look away from each other and reveal themselves in different roles; and the direct speech of both these secondary characters provides fresh comparisons by which we can perhaps hear more in Julian and Maddalo's own voices: more, not only of their disagreement, but also of the shifting extent to which it is Maddalo who might turn out to be the sentimentalist and Julian the pragmatic man of affairs.

However, the Madman is originally introduced as a means of clarifying a clear difference of opinion. For Byron, the idea that 'love, beauty and truth' were to be sought 'in our mind' (lines 174–5) merely encouraged fantasy. In *Childe Harolde*, he describes Art's imagining of ideals that never had – and never would have – equivalents in the real world as virtually a mental illness: 'a mind diseased' that 'fevers into false creation'. The ardent pursuit of true love and beauty is, for Byron, a pathological refusal to grow up: 'Who loves, raves – 'tis youth's frenzy'. Carrying on such aspirations through maturity could prove traumatizing, reducing the once optimistic idealist to a raving lunatic.[1]

Do you think that Maddalo's chosen example of a 'mind diseased', in the Madman, is fair to the Shelleyan position? The Madman indeed 'loves, raves'. But perhaps he seems so obsessed with his own frustrated desire for one idealized woman that he embodies a misleadingly narrow-minded version of Julian's 'love, beauty and truth'. Notice the emphasis on an italicized *'me'* in lines 442 and 449 and the repeated use of 'I' throughout: at one point it appears, within a mere ten lines, no less than seven times (lines 494–503).

Julian's hopes sound less egotistical. He uses plural pronouns – 'we', 'our', 'us' – when expressing concern for all humanity (lines 170–6 and 180–90). The madman, 'when a boy', perhaps *'did devote'* himself 'to justice' as well as 'to love' (lines 380–81). And he may still ramble into a few, perfunctory gestures about 'tyranny' (lines 362–3) and his own sensitivity to 'oppressions' imposed on others – 'the poor and trampled' or 'the captive'. But the self-congratulation of such moments does not take us far from his customary self-pity (lines 442–50).

Julian accepts his own part in a corporate responsibility, blaming misery and oppression on 'man's own wilful ill'. The Madman, by contrast, in spite of his claimed freedom from any desire for 'revenge' (line 366, lines 493–4), often blames the woman who has failed to love him (lines 337–43, 384–90, 398–407). And, when he wonders about the sources of more widespread unhappiness, he can only express bafflement: 'What Power delights to torture us?' (line 320). This perhaps confesses the very deficiency that Julian had anticipated: 'a want of . . . *theory*' (line 203). The Madman – so proud of recognizing how 'worthless' he is (line 383), so competitive in his assertion of unique self-abasement ('Never one/ Humbled himself before, as I have done', lines 410–11) may exemplify those prevailing conventions of thought and language which sanctify despair. But what he so typically embodies, he cannot analyse.

Shelley would argue that, if we are ever to change our world, the rhetoric in which we think and feel must change too. So, the disruptive clash of different kinds of discourse in 'Julian and Maddalo' has point. The Madman's speech is jarringly distinct from the urbane introduction. It may sometimes seem incomprehensible. But then he has not accepted the poet's responsibility to make sense for a larger audience.

Maddalo surely cheats in claiming this almost autistic figure as an archetype of poets. Such a deviant example may actually undermine the view which it is intended to support: that worthwhile verse is born of 'suffering' rather than Shelleyan optimism (544–6). In fact, the Madman's undisciplined ramblings are a letter to no-one but himself. At the one point where he is explicit about having pen in hand, his ubiquitous despair extends to discovering hopelessness in language too: 'vain . . . words . . . charactered in vain' (lines 377–8). The 'wild language of his grief' might have been 'called poetry' if it had been 'in measure'; but it is not (lines 541–2).

Julian, by contrast, is a self-portrait of the poet who is capable of writing this very work. Yet, he must adapt his poem's voice to include the reported speech of an almost incoherent lunatic. He must also respond to a contrasting pressure: the temptation to write (and perhaps, in a sense, to live) in that elegant style favoured by his supposed opponent, Maddalo: a style implicitly validated by the setting of Venice.

In the light of these twin pressures, please now reconsider the poem's final movement towards its fragmented close (lines 547–617).

DISCUSSION

The temptation to remain 'in Maddalo's great palace', reverencing the traditional cultural heritage of Venice and viewing life in terms of individual sensibility, is still strong in lines 547–83. Books, pictures, statues and, above all, conversation with that one close, highly refined friend, would sanction an introspective concern with singular selfhood: Maddalo's 'wit/ And subtle talk would . . . make me know *myself*' (lines 559–61). These enticements would innately support an act of private charity to the Madman: one intriguingly singular victim to be reclaimed 'from his dark estate' (line 574): rather than an entire community of the mystified to be rescued from 'their dark lot' (line 112).

Those temptations, however, are surely resisted: at least in terms of symbolic narrative, if not at the level of poetic style. For

Julian, such 'dreams of baseless good' evaporate (lines 578–80). He is not 'an unconnected man' (line 547). He has 'friends in London' (line 564). He leaves Venice, 'urged . . . by affairs' (lines 582–3). These, though the poem does not describe them, could reflect the more communal values that he had articulated before being distracted by Maddalo's ploy of introducing the Madman. Certainly they lead, for 'many years', to a life elsewhere. That life allows, or even achieves, 'many changes': far away from the allurements of 'bright Venice' (lines 583–4).

The charms of elegant, ancient Venice are explicitly and specifically urban (lines 556–8). For them, the urbane form of the heroic couplet seems appropriate. This seems less well-suited to Julian's almost uncontrollable anger at the architecture of religious oppression. For instance, his bitter exclamation in lines 111–13, in its compression and distorted word-order, can sound close to hysteria. But perhaps it is an almost envious anticipation of that freedom to disrupt linguistic decorum which the Madman enjoys and will soon exhibit. The frequent ellipses in the Madman's speeches may suggest a mind that defiantly gives itself more spaces in which to manoeuvre than traditional logic would permit.

Certainly there is, from the outset, an implicit dissatisfaction with the conventional role of the poet. In his description of Julian in the Preface, what Shelley does include transparently indicates a self-portrait. So, the omission of any hint that Julian might also be a writer makes a loud silence. At the other end of the work, Shelley refuses to perform the story-teller's professional duty of tidying all those disparate voices down into any neat narrative closure. His mouthpiece, Julian, ultimately abandons any attempt to pass on what Maddalo's daughter has taught him; even though she is a figure as 'transcendent' as 'one of Shakespeare's women' (lines 591–2). The poem refuses to convey any reductive lesson. Nor will it show any imitative respect for the tradition that Shakespeare represents by granting its own heroine, or indeed any of its characters, a decisive ending, let alone a happy one.

We ourselves, as frustrated readers of a story, are treated no less harshly than that undeservingly 'cold world' who 'shall not know'. We are accused of being part of a beau monde, whose taste for tales of passion is as comfortably dilettantist as our pleasure in 'books . . . Pictures . . . statues fair' (lines 554–5). But these, of course, are what Julian himself has confessed to finding all too arresting earlier.

The secretive conclusion could be intended as a merely piquant tease. If so, you could enjoy it as the last sparkle of a dazzling fireworks display; or you may resent it as an ill-chosen, damp squib. But the shan't-tell ending is perhaps aimed more seriously: inviting us to wonder what more we want to know and why.

Are we so sure that it's the Madman we want to hear more

about, rather than, for instance, the mysteriously absent Maddalo? His purpose in travelling 'far away/ Among the mountains of Armenia' is firmly withheld from us: a tantalising contrast to our being granted the surely useless information that 'His dog was dead' (lines 586–8). And should we not be at least as curious about what 'affairs' with 'friends in London' have kept Julian so busy that he now seems an old man: complete with 'wrinkled cheeks' and the pompous tendency to address someone, who has visibly 'now become/ A woman', as 'Child' (lines 582, 564, 612, 588–9, 608).

Perhaps the poem – with all its sly evasiveness and disconcerting range of tones – suggests that, if new ideas are to be articulated, we must challenge those structures in which society has traditionally shaped its stories to reflect its own values. Perhaps, too, more specific conventions of poetic genre and style would need to be defied.

Yet such structures and conventions provide the only available resources by which a poet can hope to sound intelligible to his contemporary readers. Even the greatest writers, the Preface to *Prometheus Unbound* argues, must deploy the terminology of their times:

> It is true that, not the spirit of their genius, but the forms in which it has manifested itself, are due less to the peculiarities of their own minds than to the peculiarity of the moral and intellectual condition of the minds among which they have been produced.   (Webb, p. 31)

An absolutely new style, even if a time-bound author could invent it, would be as meaningless to its readers as a foreign language that they had never heard before.

So Shelley's strategy is often to juxtapose conventional genres and tones in *un*conventional combinations. Great poems seem 'beautiful and new', he argues, 'not because the portions of which they are composed had no previous existence . . . but because [of] the whole produced by their combination' (Webb, pp. 31–2). Since 'every man's mind . . . is modified . . . by every word and every suggestion which he ever admitted to act upon his consciousness', even the greatest writer is an essentially 'combined product'. He may have 'such internal powers as modify the nature of others'. But he is himself also composed of essentially 'external influences'. So, 'Poets . . . are in one sense, the creators, and in another, the creations, of their age' (Webb, p. 32).

The conventional literature of the Sublime, for example, had made the image of the thunderstorm an almost lifelessly inert cliché: so established that the establishment's most dedicated supporters could meet thunder and lightning, in poem after poem, without being even faintly disturbed. Yet, in Shelley's writings, the storm regains its vigour through the cunningly designed settings in which it explodes and in the dynamic combinations of clashing styles which carry it. Shelley describes the great writers of his own age as:

> forerunners of some unimagined change in our social condition or the opinions which cement it. The cloud of mind is discharging its collected lightning . . .   (Webb, p. 32)

To learn more about Shelley's challenging redeployment of conventional language, you could make your own personal anthology of Shelley's storm-images; and a similar compilation of his references to buildings, ruined or reconstructed. Typically enough, the quotation above – which combines the 'cloud of mind's' discharged 'lightning' with that carefully chosen verb, 'cement' – may, like the storm-surrounded architecture of 'Julian and Maddalo', belong in both collections.[2]

Shelley is not for the tidy-minded. At best, his poetry does, however obscurely, overcome its dependence on traditional forms. It subverts their innately conservative associations; and manages, in defiance of logic, to image that as yet 'unimagined change'.

I hope to show both the unified strategy and the varying tactics of Shelley's campaign to change our minds by now moving on to the second of our 'love and politics' poems: *Epipsychidion*.

Perhaps the most recurrent challenge of Shelley's verse is its insistence that we break down the mental divisions into which, at present, we allocate our experience. The passionately specific love that in 'Julian and Maddalo' has led to madness and imprisonment recurs as a central theme of *Epipsychidion*; but here, such love is frequently celebrated as a source of sanity and liberation. That liberation is partly social. Sexual love and political reform are topics that our minds might normally keep quite separate, in such safely sterile compartments that no cross-fertilization can occur. You should be able to notice, even on a first reading, some of the ways that *Epipsychidion* attempts to dissolve these boundaries. But you can also practise on the perhaps easier ground of the borders between 'love' and 'friendship'. The poem asks us to consider these terms in closer proximity than convention encourages. For this, pay particular attention when you come to lines 150–60. Please read the poem now.

DISCUSSION

Shelley's poetry of liberation aims to begin its work by liberating its own readers. So it does not seek to impose some instantaneous change in what they consciously believe about some specific issue of politics or religion or ethics. What the verse seeks in its readers is not acquiescence but alertness.

Concepts and terms whose neutrality is too often taken for
granted are probed by the verse until they are shown to raise
questions of value; but just how these questions are best answered
remains each reader's responsibility. 'Didactic poetry', Shelley protests, is his 'abhorrence' since anything that 'can be equally well
expressed in prose' is 'tedious and superogatory in verse' ('Preface' to
Prometheus Unbound, Webb, p. 32). A poem like *Epipsychidion*
thus demands not only flexibly open minds but also attentively open
ears. Its argument is poetic argument, manipulating sound to define
sense.

Consider, for instance, that famous rejection of monogamous
marriage:

> I never was attached to that great sect,
> Whose doctrine is, that each one should select
> Out of the crowd, a mistress or a friend,
> And all the rest, though fair and wise, commend
> To cold oblivion, though it is in the code
> Of modern morals, and the beaten road
> Which those poor slaves with weary footsteps tread,
> Who travel to their home among the dead
> By the broad highway of the world, and so
> With one chained friend, perhaps a jealous foe,
> The dreariest and longest journey go.

> *   *   *

> Narrow
> The heart that loves, the brain that contemplates,
> The life that wears, the spirit that creates
> One object, and one form, and builds thereby
> A sepulchre for its eternity.   (lines 150–60)

Such verse poses an undisguised challenge to conformist attitudes.
However, it does not try to bully us, as readers. It seeks to persuade.
It abandons any claims to special authority: the word 'I' reminds us
that we are listening to just one person's point of view. Moreover,
this person is audibly not the kind of élitist who condemns the mass
of people as vulgar. The collective nouns of 'crowd' and 'world' are
posed in opposition. The 'crowd' is apparently not a faceless mob;
but a multiplicity of individuals whom a generously affectionate
person would wish to keep as friends, rather than consign to 'cold
oblivion'. By contrast, 'the world' (which perhaps has derogatory
associations with the 'beau monde') is mocked. So too perhaps is the
church: the teasing use of religious terms like 'doctrine' and 'sect'
suggests that it is largely Christian indoctrination that keeps most
'poor slaves' to the 'beaten road' of monogamy.

We are not invited to despise marriage *per se*; but rather, a
mindless acceptance of established forms on no better grounds than
their respectable image in the eyes of some 'great sect'. A 'doctrine' or

a 'code' is not an unquestionable absolute that applies at all times in all societies. If marriage is the transient, localized structure 'Of *modern* morals', unthinking acceptance of it narrows the mind, blinkering us to alternative paths, as if England in the early nineteenth century is 'the world' as it must always be.

Shelley's choice of words here reveals how often words can stultify rather than stimulate thought. 'Home', in the vocabulary of a society grounded upon the nuclear family, has cosy connotations of unchanging stability. Yet a 'home among the dead' reminds us that permanence is not always and everywhere desirable. Stillness does not evoke security if it is caused by imprisonment ('chained') or by death ('sepulchre'). Change and variety need not suggest danger and confusion if they welcome a whole 'crowd' of the 'fair and wise'.

Alternative terms invite readers to choose their own definitions – 'a mistress or a friend', 'one chained friend, perhaps a jealous foe'. That one term, 'mistress', though implying here some sort of sexual choice, can itself have a number of distinct connotations ranging from the reverently romantic to the patronisingly lecherous; but how compatible are any of those associations with simple friendliness? And should a wife feel flattered or insulted to have been selected on the same grounds as would apply in choosing a 'mistress or a friend'?

The repetition of 'friend' challenges us to connect two values which we normally keep in separate compartments: friendship on the one hand, marriage on the other. Conventional morality might claim to value both; but conventional language prefers to keep their vocabularies quite distinct.

For instance, the emphasis here on the singular case ('*a* friend', '*one* friend', '*one* object and *one* form'), can seem odd in a culture which suggests that friends should be, almost by definition, plural. To have only one friend might seem, at best, extraordinarily unlucky; and, at worst, so unnatural as to mean one was abusing the language in describing that relationship as merely a friendship. Yet, where 'a mistress or a friend' are ways of describing a wife, to expect any other case than the singular would be to flirt with bigamy.

The image of life as a journey may seem comfortably familiar in the plural world of friends: consider the travelling companions that throng works like *Pilgrim's Progress* or *The Canterbury Tales*. Yet that same image of travel can, in the singular world of monogamous marriage, seem disconcertingly odd. In that context, relationship tends to be defined through quite opposed imagery where the ideal is staying put in one, unchanging 'home'. How compatible are the ways in which we define our faith in friendship and our respect for marriage?

Shelley's language thus poses questions. It asks us to spell out the surreptitious implications of our various beliefs, the ways in which they may tacitly contradict each other. It does not seek to replace one set of prejudices with another; but to be curious about the value-laden terms in which we think and speak.

Poetry, of course, is that kind of literature which most obviously asks to be spoken aloud; and you can use this passage to explore the advantages of listening to, and not just looking at, Shelley's verse. Try reading it out loud now before considering my own comments on its use of sound below. Listen to the demands of syntax, particularly sentence-length, as well as the patterning required by the use of rhyme.

DISCUSSION

The first sentence is unusually long; it is sustained for eleven lines. The lines rhyme in pairs; but then the pattern expands at the sentence's end so that the long vowels of 'so', 'foe', 'go' toll out a treble warning. The sentence is about length and it is about linking. It evokes 'the longest journey' of a traveller tied to 'one chained friend'. So both the stamina and the self-discipline required in the reading voice, if one is to maintain the sense and to articulate that interlocking pattern of rhyme, are appropriately demanding.

Rhyming words, so audibly yoked by sound, may invite one to consider whether their meanings too, however surprisingly, belong together. Attachment to a multitudinous 'sect', for instance, is paradoxically to be isolated as just 'one' who must 'select'; to 'narrow the heart' until it focuses exclusively on 'One object'.

What at first sounds like a rational 'code' of proper behaviour is then revealed as chiming precisely with the irrational conformity of a well-trodden 'road'. The superficially active victims that 'tread' such a road anticipate the stationary 'dead' whom they will join at its end. The sense of being lured further and further down a bleak cul-de-sac may be reinforced by the fact that the 'code'/'road' pair is immediately followed by the 'tread'/'dead' pair. The variation of vowel-sounds between these two pairs sounds a feeble freedom, confined as it is by the quadruple reiteration of the 'd' consonant which closes all four words.

At the beginnings of words too, consonants play their part. The 'code of modern morals' is a phrase which makes its scorn audible through the alliterative repetition of its dismissive 'm' sounds.

Moreover, long words support the implications of that long sentence in which they are deployed: the superlatives of 'the dreariest and the longest' arrest the ear, intervening before we can reach the noun which they qualify, and so forcing us to hear how wearyingly long such a trek can feel.

The sombre threat which is the poetry's message here is a

recurring note in Shelley. The oppression which he saw in contemporary society is often presented as appallingly wasteful. But that bitter sense of waste is seldom far away in his verse from some insistently positive evocation of all that we could be if only we could nerve ourselves to change.

Typically, the lines that we have been considering are lodged in a portion of *Epipsychidion* where that work is most obviously a passionate love-poem. It is equally characteristic that such bitter lines are immediately juxtaposed in the full poem with a defiantly optimistic prophecy that 'True Love' will inevitably emerge triumphant for some future generation. Meanwhile, for Shelley's own generation, there is work to be done. Firstly, 'this world of life', though at present so undeniably 'ravaged' by the repressive forces who are now in control, must be recognized as innately good: an Eden-like 'garden', deformed only for a while into a jungle of competitive greed. Secondly, that change which will reveal the underlying glory of human potential must not be passively awaited, but actively pursued. A combative commitment is needed to those

> . . . whose strife
> Tills for the promise of a later birth
> The wilderness of this Elysian earth.   (lines 187–9)

Please look again at the longer sequence which interweaves these rousing lines with the far more ominous extract we were considering earlier. Begin reading at line 142 ('We – are we not formed . . .') and go on until at least line 216 ('. . . the harmony of truth.'). Consider what this sequence suggests about Shelley's attitudes to the possibility of change, his sense of the ways in which the present can be related both to the past and to the future.

DISCUSSION

One editor glosses the 'shattered present' (line 212) as 'the random experience of everyday current activity';[3] but surely Shelley here is thinking more precisely. It is only in peculiarly turbulent times that people are likely to feel every day that they are living through a 'Storm' so shattering that it 'chokes the past'.

Shelley may well have thought that his generation was having to endure just such times: The French Revolution, the Napoleonic wars and the violently repressive regimes with which the reactionary victors of those wars sought to resist any further attempts at political change. If so, the past that can hardly breathe in the present climate may recall that 'garden ravaged' still recognized by the 'sages' of lines 184–9: their Eden-like ideal of human affection whose flowers, for the time being, must struggle almost helplessly in a smothering 'wilderness'.

There *are*, of course, 'flowers' in the ensuing description of that 'Being' who Shelley himself remembers (lines 190–216) – or at least their remembered 'odours deep' (lines 202–3); and what these recalled smells evoke are 'lips murmuring in their sleep': lips that themselves sleepily remember 'kisses'; and these remembered kisses in turn recall '*her*': the ideal 'Being' of line 190. But she is recalled only through these elaborate Chinese boxes of somnolent memories hidden deep within other memories. So, that present participle of 'Being' is scarcely appropriate for what is an almost irrecoverable past: 'Her Spirit *was* . . .' (line 216).

The poetry here seems so concerned to evoke its own difficulties in recovering the ideals of an earlier time that it cannot consistently offer any precise definition of what it seeks to recall. Indeed, Timothy Webb has argued:

> The whole of *Epipsychidion* is a self-conscious and highly wrought piece of art; indeed, to a much greater extent than most of Shelley's other poems, it is a poem about the difficulties involved in its own composition. The ebb and flow of inspiration is deliberately exploited as a structural principle; the apparent lack of unity is the result of a calculated attempt to reproduce the very process of creation.[4]

Yet there is indeed 'flow' as well as 'ebb' here. We can deduce some of the ideals represented by this elusive 'Being' from the fluent assertions about 'True Love' and the power of the 'Mind' in lines 160–8 and lines 174–89.

These most confidently taught lessons must be what the poet himself learnt from a more optimistic past that preceded the muffling effects of the present 'Storm'. Indeed, at the beginning of our extract, he feels a momentary union with a feminine ideal whose value he must recognize because of what that earlier 'Being' once taught him to value. The repeated 'We . . . we' of line 142 insists on this union, however precarious; and at line 147, the poet claims that the 'wisdom' of the woman he now loves 'speaks in' the proud lines with which he then denounces the narrow-hearted possessiveness of conventional relationship.

Later, in lines 190–216, the ideal is a far more elusive figure haunting a past which, even at the time, was so 'fairy' and 'enchanted' (lines 193, 194), so blurred with 'sleep' and 'dream' (lines 195, 196), so 'imagined' (line 197) that the poet, though 'met' by her (line 199) cannot claim to have seen her: 'I beheld her not' (line 200).

Yet the ensuing lines proceed to sketch in quite enough about this more inspiring past for us to tell it clearly apart from the 'shattered present'. The 'breezes' and 'the singing of the summer birds' (lines 206, 208) which are components in the 'voice' of the past (line 201) are clearly opposed to the present 'Storm'. And that remembered voice, with its 'fountains' and 'flowers' and 'kisses' (lines 202, 203, 204) is what the present, in its most brutally repressive moments, 'chokes'. This last word seems to me wonderfully economic. The struggle between the 'Storm/ Which . . . *chokes*' and 'whatever' echoes of the past's voice still '*checks*' its destructiveness is audible in the shifting vowel which is all that distinguishes the interlocked combatants. And 'chokes' is such a versatile term in being so brutally, physically apt: whether we apply its smothering pressure to the 'voice' and 'lips murmuring . . . Of . . . kisses'; or to the 'fountains'; or to the fertility of that 'garden' which is being 'ravaged' into a 'wilderness' (lines 187–9).

Shelley's interest in 'the words/ Of antique verse and high romance' (lines 209–10) is more than the merely professional one of a craftsman who works in verse and finds it useful to study the technical tricks of his predecessors. The search for some 'form,/ Sound, colour' (lines 210–11) in which his poetry could articulate a more optimistic view of the ideals that have inspired the French Revolution was for him an urgent, political necessity. Cynicism about such ideals was so widespread at the time that the then dominant patterns of 'form,/ Sound' constituted a medium in which the message of radical optimism would be subverted. Only a reaching far back – perhaps as far as the pre-Christian myths of Eden and the Elysian fields of classical myth – could allow any movement forward from the stasis of the present's 'cold common hell' (line 214).

So Shelley's 'best philosophy' here, though its inspiration is like some 'glorious . . . fiery martyrdom', is not a support for, but a defiant challenge to, that Christianity which was telling the poor that their suffering was meaningful to God and would be rewarded in some after-life elsewhere. It is not some remote Heaven but 'this . . . earth' and 'this . . . our life' upon it (lines 189, 214) that concerns Shelley, whether he is focusing on its hellish actuality in the 'shattered present' or on its 'Elysian' potential for some 'later birth'.

The arduous 'strife' that 'Tills . . . this . . . earth' for some future fertility is thus partly a process of revision: a re-writing of the language in which we think and act so that a proper definition of 'True Love' can be born again. Negatively, it involves detaching oneself from 'that great sect' described in lines 149–59 and 169–73. Positively, it embraces the love offered in lines 142–8 and described in lines 160–9 as well as the limitlessly expanding Mind that is defined and exercised in lines 174–89.

Generous love and expansive thought are, of course, almost inextricably entwined here. Consider, for instance, line 180 where 'pleasure and love and thought' are listed even-handedly. We hardly need to know that Shelley had originally written 'Free Love' rather than 'True love' in line 161 to guess that 'pleasure', in this context, must include the erotic, must celebrate that spontaneous, unrestricted sexuality which 'modern morals' (line 156) seek to repress. But the addition of the two other terms – 'love and thought' – insists that the truly affectionate mind, though nurtured by sharing pleasures that are sexual, will grow to embrace a much broader definition of love: one that can operate in far from erotic situations.

To see what I mean, you should now read two, relatively lightweight, poems on which I will not be offering a detailed discussion. Each of them was written in response to a specific – and potentially enraging – occasion. Both are addressed to males; and both explicitly wrestle with the temptation to 'hate'. Yet, you may agree that both could be included in an anthology of Shelley's love poetry; that both contribute to the extraordinarily far-reaching definition of 'True love' that Shelley's verse attempts.

Please read first 'Lines to a Critic' (Webb, p. 90; Note, p. 207); and then 'To the Lord Chancellor' (Webb, p. 9; Note, p. 193). You will find it useful, in both cases, to have looked at Webb's introductory note about the context of each before reading it.

DISCUSSION

In both poems, Shelley attempts to describe – and then to transcend – a potentially endless cycle of hatred. This cycle is what delays the needed change in human nature: that transformation in our attitudes to each other without which society can never be truly transformed. In delineating the vicious circle, both poems deploy a favourite Shelleyan paradox: the bully and the bullied are on the same conservative side.

The 'slave of power and gold' (in 'Lines to a Critic', line 10) could be a mighty tyrant, enslaved in his addiction to prestige and material wealth; or he could be a typical subject of such a tyrant: so politically impotent and so economically deprived that he must play the part of a literal slave. Either of these may feel unalterable hatred for each other and thus be 'that bigot cold' (line 11), doomed 'to repay' endlessly the bitterness of the other with 'An equal passion'; just as each would reciprocate the critic's hostility, surrendering to the same futile, negative emotions that had led the critic to his attack.

From such sterile interchange, there can never grow that fertile transformation which Shelley would define as true change. So he must 'prove' his own genuine opposition to both these mock-opponents. He must demonstrate his 'passion' for 'truth and love' by refusing to divide humanity into those who deserve his hatred and those who have earned some meanly selective version of a love that scarcely deserves the name (lines 13–16). To pigeon-hole others so divisively would be to divide and conquer his own best self.

Even more explicitly, 'To the Lord Chancellor' enacts this process of self-disciplining, self-preserving redefinition. The seemingly potent 'Tyrant' addressed with what sounds like hatred in line 60 is then recognized as a pathetic 'slave' in the next line; and he is offered, in the poem's closing phrase, a 'Fare thee well' which is not just a dismissive good-bye or a sarcasm. It is also a gesture of affection. This gesture may be but one competing ingredient in a complex of meanings and it certainly flickers into precarious life only as the poem is anyway about to close.

But Shelley does not mean to make it sound easy. Both poems do more than just expose the folly of their embittered addresses. They also evoke the poet's own difficulty in restraining himself from joining in such folly. We must at first struggle to use the new, alien-sounding syntax of generosity with the same clumsiness and lack of stamina with which we would speak any tongue foreign to our upbringing: love learnt as a second language. Indeed, what such poems do mean to evoke as all too easy is the glib fluency with which we can all relax back into the familiar grammar of hate.

In our next poem, 'Ozymandias', we find again the loveless rhetoric of self-love, the egotistical obsession with one's own illusory power (or with equally deluded beliefs in one's *lack* of power). Here, a long-dead tyrant's fantasy that he could resist all change, and would eternally intimidate his enemies, has been transformed into a monumental irony: a lasting statement that the only certainties are the inevitability of change and the ultimate helplessness of all such megalomaniac dictators. But, around this simple reversal, the poem weaves an elaborate network of ambiguities.

Read it now (Webb, p. 11), trying to identify for yourself the enigmatic components with which it invites you to play.

Then, please consider these questions:

1 Do you find Shelley's style here obscure? Specifically, how would you sort out the syntax of lines 6–8?
   One editor glosses them thus:

   > The Phrase, 'stamped on these lifeless things', is almost parentheti-
   > cal, identifying the medium through which the 'passions' survive
   > (outlive) the sculptor's hand. The sculptor's 'hand mocked' (imi-
   > tated and derided) the 'passions' that Ozymandias' 'heart fed'.[5]

   Does this omit implications which are at least as interesting?
2 Is the sonnet sometimes just restating the obvious? For instance, does the third line's 'in the desert . . . on the sand' make the last line's description of 'lone . . . sands' superfluous? And are those

sands called, not only 'boundless and bare', but also 'lone and level' simply because the sonnet needs padding if it is to complete its metrical pattern?

3　Ozymandias intended the statement inscribed on his statue's pedestal to last; and, as a sequence of words, now wholly divorced from the meaning he intended, they do (lines 10–11). The name that he so confidently announced in the opening clause of that inscription is now intriguing, precisely because its exotic-sounding syllables trigger no memories; and, as such, it is deployed to govern the entire poem as the work's arrestingly mysterious title. This word is in fact the Greek version of the name of Rameses II, who died in 1234 B.C. So, for Shelley's first readers, three thousand years have passed when 'a traveller' reads the words of that inscription and reports them to the poet. The king has turned himself into an inscribed text (the words 'on the pedestal'); which itself has become a traveller's tale; which, in turn, passes into a poet's memory; which is then shaped into a printed text; which is now, after another one and a half centuries have passed, still being read.

How does the interdependence of so many texts and the passage of so much time colour our response, not only to the inscription, but also to the poem's, overall story: a story which begins so decisively ('I met') and yet ends so elusively ('far away')?

DISCUSSION

1　There are, surely, other fruitful ways of reading lines 6–8.

Prudent courtiers flatter a tyrant. So, Ozymandias' megalomania may have been nourished by the apparent respect of those who sought his patronage. That vanity, which is the 'heart' of his 'passions', may have 'fed' on what he took to be the sculptor's heart-felt admiration. It was, after all, the sculptor who made 'these words appear'. It was his self-effacing labour and skill which represented this worthless little bully as some omnipotent 'king of kings'; and described Ozymandias' achievements as such that others could only 'despair'. Shelley frequently insists that those who despair of their own worth and behave as if they were powerless in fact carve out the confidence and power of those who exploit them. They themselves write the script which allows a fellow human being to play God.

Yet the physiological context ('trunkless legs', 'lip', 'hand') allows us to take literally both 'heart' (on whose repeated beat every continuing second of a human life depends); and 'fed' (as implying no more, and no less, than that palpable nourishment without which we die of starvation). The sculptor, whose very survival depended on continuing to please his ruthless patron, may have felt that, between a flattery which earned a meal-ticket and a refusal which might provoke a summary death-sentence, he had no real choice.

Might 'stamped on' hint at the sculptor's repressed hatred, his secret wish to trample under foot the tyrant that he must pretend to admire? If so, the sculptor's self-abasement may have 'fed' the 'passions' of political absolutism in his own brutalized 'heart'. His secret resentment may have nurtured murderous fantasies of one day being able to issue his own 'cold command'. He may have 'read' the cruel language of power all too 'well'. The one example we have of his writing in that language, does after all make him virtually claim that his own 'name is Ozymandias'.

The oppressed, according to a Shelleyan view of history, have too often learnt only to hate their oppressors. They have 'fed' upon the same corrupting passions as those they would overthrow. The down-trodden may rebel, as so recently in France, abandoning their own servility; but only to adopt in turn the same malicious scorn and to seek servility in others.

Shelley's interest in the ruins of the ancient world taught him that the grandiose monuments of each defeated empire, sneeringly 'stamped on' by the victors, had soon been replaced by an all too similar iconography of arrogance. Eventually, this sequence in which no real change occurs had produced those modern tyrannies which, for Shelley's first readers, visibly 'yet survive' in post-war Europe. Such dictatorships, in their greedy *hubris*, were locked in those same, arid 'passions' that were still creating only a wasteland of sterility and despair: still turning the potential garden of human society into a loveless desert.

The sculptor's 'heart' may have been corrupted by a diet of clandestine bitterness until he and Ozymandias are morally indistinguishable. Or he may have seen that risk in time, reading his own propensity for such passions well enough to evade them. He may, with conscious irony, have designed his work of art to mock dictatorship without hating or wishing to become the dictator.

Certainly, we ourselves are meant to read beyond any such sterile exchanges of ambition: to stamp out our tendency to respect monuments of authoritarianism without longing to stamp upon the people who made them. If we use the poem's liberatingly mobile syntax to recognize and escape our own tendency to hate, then we may be able to dismantle those intellectual patterns of servility and scorn which maintain the symbiotic relationship of ruled and ruler.

2 You could argue that such repetitive terminology is well suited to this bleakly monotonous landscape. But this terrain, for all its apparent lack of variation, in fact proves that long-term change is

inevitable. The 'level' sands of time are actively levelling and expunging all distinction between the most apparently distinguished 'king of kings' and the humbly anonymous craftsman who carved his statues. Similarly, 'boundless' could be cheeringly expansive, encouraging our own minds to 'stretch far away', reaching beyond all that our current, hierarchical assumptions define as reasonable bounds, until we can conceive some new, more egalitarian, society.

Yet the poem also acknowledges that, for the time being, we must see present pathos, as well as latent power, in the human condition, focusing more on the mortality of each person than on the longevity of the human species. The adjectives 'bare' and 'lone' suggest a more vulnerably exposed individuality; and it is not just the sneering king, but also the perhaps pluckily satirical artist who has been dead and forgotten for centuries.

The dead sculptor – and indeed the mortal poet composing this sonnet – could borrow Ozymandias' words and put them to consciously poignant use: 'Look on my works . . . and despair'. Of the people they once were, 'Nothing beside remains' – only these fading artefacts, 'these lifeless things', which one day – in some 'boundless . . . far away' future, may disappear completely beneath the sands of time.

3 The series of Chinese boxes through which Ozymandias' inscription reaches us could suggest that his is not the only statement that is over-optimistic about its own longevity. Perhaps the sonnet's own briskly informative opening may itself have been guilty of undue confidence in the stability of the meanings that it has to offer.

The poem which, by the end, is knowingly a puzzle, may imply that the relationship between any text and the passage of time is highly puzzling. The poetic structure of this sonnet could itself appear, to each succeeding generation, as crumbling into a yet more inaccessibly fragmented form. Its significance, as the centuries pass, could change almost as much as that of the inscription which Ozymandias so rashly chose for conveying his power to future readers. The sonnet's own signs too could theoretically end up being stranded in some context which produces meanings utterly opposed to those that had first been intended. Perhaps the poem does anticipate the gradual disintegration of its own import – 'Half sunk . . . shattered' – until posterity regards it as a mere curio: the scarcely articulate relic of a lost civilization whose style of thought may have become almost unimaginable. Certainly, the sonnet begins by announcing that its traveller's tale derives from an already ancient country. In doing so, it deploys what, even at the time of composition, was becoming a quaintly outmoded usage of 'antique': as if to suggest that its manner, like its message, may become an anachronism.

A surprising proportion of the terminology is, after all, devoted to emphasizing the simple fact of ruinous change – 'trunkless', 'Half sunk', 'shattered', 'decay', 'wreck'. Is this just verbosity? Or is it an effectively relentless series of hammer-blows with which to demolish the stony pretensions of all texts which seek to intimidate us by claiming to have crystallized some immutable truth?

The poem obviously relishes its task of dismantling the pretensions of Ozymandias' inscription. May it not assemble out of the resulting debris a self-destruct mechanism to ensure that it cannot itself ever be despised as blind to the 'bare' fact that massive change, in whatever direction, will come? Its knowing ignorance may 'stretch far away', gesturing towards all those future contexts which it cannot imagine in detail but which it knows could well supply bizarrely different readings.

You may feel that this chapter concentrates too much on Shelley's doubts about poetry itself or on his hopes for a profound political change; and that the topic of love, at least in a narrow definition of that term, has been given short shrift. So, let us end by looking briefly at two poems that focus more exclusively on love-affairs.

Please read first the lyric that begins 'One word is too often profaned/ For me to profane it' (Webb, p. 164). Here, the much abused term that the poem will not itself espouse is obviously 'love'; and the poet implicitly claims to feel for the poem's addressee more, not less, than the words 'I love you' might convey. He also fears that so candid a declaration might provoke the desired woman to dash his hopes and reveal that she can only offer 'pity', not a reciprocal passion.

However, to review some of the claims I have made earlier about Shelley's expansive redefinition of the term 'love', you might also consider an alternative approach. How would this poem, to which Shelley in fact gave no title, read if it were headed 'Hymn to Intellectual Beauty'; or even 'Ode to Liberty'? I am not being so perverse as to suggest that here the suppressed term which has been 'too often profaned' should be understood as 'revolution', rather than 'love'. But you may agree that at least the second and last stanza would make complete sense under either of my hypothetical titles. And Shelley actually gave each of those titles to lines which, if about erotic affection at all, are clearly far more concerned with other aspirations.

Interpreted straightforwardly, this is a poem about a love-affair which has not yet started. After it, please move on to 'When Passion's Trance is Overpast' (Webb, p. 163), Shelley's poignant account of an affair where the love is already finished. Here, the poet's attempt to offer at least friendliness and candour where he can no longer offer passion is threatened by 'wild feelings'. But do these 'fires unseen' derive from memories of a past more happily shared or from clandestine hopes of a future separation and a wholly new love? For me, this poem's majestic simplicity of craftmanship falters when its third and final stanza turns to focus on less bitterly specific transience. But then any lines might seem anticlimactic after the economy of the first two stanzas. These contrive to press movingly intense experience from the very inability to feel intensely. If this represents a strand of Shelley's verse that you want to pursue further, you will also enjoy 'Stanzas Written in Dejection' (Webb, p. 11).

Learning to feel with sufficient intensity and generosity is, Shelley's verse suggests, crucial. Its energetic redefinitions imply that true love would not confine us in a few narrowly exclusive relationships but liberate our capacity to care about, and to change, our entire society. Yet the difficulty of accepting and acting upon such a lesson is frequently demonstrated through the poet's evocations of his own inadequacy. The self-portrait in 'Julian and Maddalo' confesses the ease with which Shelley's own poetry could become as ineffectual as either Maddalo's urbane cynicism or the Madman's more inarticulate emotionalism. *Epipsychidion* records its own tendency to an idealization which is dangerously close to escapism. In 'Ozymandias', the sculptor represents a profoundly ambiguous portrait of the artist. Here, as in the poems to the Lord Chancellor or the Critic, the obligation of the creative artist to love his enemy may be clear. But Shelley evokes at least as clearly the poet's own difficulty in designing an artefact which can articulate such forgiveness, while still telling the truth about injustice. That becomes an even more urgent problem for the more topical, more obviously political poems which we will consider in the next chapter.

Meanwhile, you might look back on this chapter and consider whether 'Love and *Poetry*' might not have been as apt a title as 'Love and Politics'. Shelley tends to be such a self-conscious artist that any group of his poems is likely to reveal his recurrent insistence on both the limitations and the importance of poetry. But, poetry's importance ultimately depends, for Shelley, on inspiring emotions that can effect social change. So in poems that seek to define that love which could be truly revolutionary, there is an unusually intense evocation of the craftsman poet's obligations; and of the technical challenges that must be overcome if they are to be fulfilled.

5. Politics and Poetry

The three poems on which we will concentrate in this chapter are 'The Mask of Anarchy', 'England in 1819' and 'Ode to the West Wind'. The first two are explicitly and specifically about contemporary politics in England. The third could be mistaken for a poem centred on the Mediterranean climate and landscape of Italy, where all three poems were written.

Shelley's fictional equivalent in 'Julian and Maddalo' has to leave his Italian host and return to 'his friends in London' (line 564). He does so reluctantly, stressing that if he were free of responsibility to others, 'an unconnected man', he would have stayed in Venice, enjoying what that ancient and foreign city offers to a refined gentleman with time on his hands. Shelley himself never did go back to England; and he uses the first line of 'The Mask' to confess that he still 'lay asleep in Italy' when the political crisis back in England reached its brutal climax in the Peterloo massacre.

Webb's introductory note to the poem (p. 200) gives some facts about this incident. But, to understand not only Shelley's disgust at the authorities' violence but also his poem's play with the concepts of Order and Anarchy, you need to understand that the demonstrators at St Peter's Field had been carefully co-ordinated to be as decorous as possible. They were, for instance, dressed in their best Sunday clothes. Each contingent had been rehearsing, for weeks beforehand, the precise order with which, at the appointed time, they would parade through Manchester, carrying their union banners and led by their bands. Their pathetic confidence that they could not be mistaken for an unruly mob and were bound to be allowed to assemble peacefully was signalled by the large proportion of children present. Of the 421 authenticated claims from those who were wounded, over 100 were from women and girls.

Conservatives had often accused the reform movement of threatening England with the 'Anarchy' that Revolution had created in France. Whenever protest could be represented as disorderly, they were loud in condemnation. Yet, secretly, they may have been relieved: a disorganized rabble posed no great threat.

So, the increasing discipline of the mass rallies that were organized, as economic conditions worsened, actually dismayed the ruling class. The general in charge of troops in the North watched an 1818 parade of strikers and then reported his anxieties about its 'peaceable demeanour': such orderly behaviour, by 'so many thousand unemployed men' was 'not natural'. A popular ballad, of the kind that Shelley's poem imitates, noted the hypocrisy exposed by such reactions to this strike:

> . . . that very ORDER they cried up before
> Did afterwards gall them ten thousand times more,
> As they found that these men, in their 'Radical Rags'
> March'd peacably on, with their Banners and Flags.[1]

After Peterloo itself, one of the magistrates recalled seeing the 'beautiful order' in which one large contingent marched into St Peter's Field and confessed that 'not until then did he become alarmed'.[2]

Peterloo, as its name – jeering at the supposed glory of Waterloo – suggests, stripped away the seemingly disciplined mask worn by Britain's militaristic government. It exposed the nation's leaders, rather than their radical opponents, as the real anarchists. It was their grisly ritual of responding to reasoned protest with chaotic violence that threatened to destroy society.

The poem's title also plays with 'Mask', as a pun. The word (even when spelt thus and not 'masque') could still in Shelley's day mean either a theatrical game, involving song and dance as well as narrative drama, played exclusively for, and often by, the aristocracy; or the form of evening party that was then so fashionable amongst England's upper classes: a masked ball. But it could also, by then, trigger its modern associations of a criminal's disguise. A government minister's use of terms like 'Anarchy' to denounce those who sought a juster society could be just like the mask worn by any other crook who meant to hide his identity and avoid being held responsible for his crimes.

Please read the poem now (Webb, p. 65).

DISCUSSION

The length of the poem may derive from its search for an adequate voice. Even when such a voice is discovered and begins to speak (at line 147), it faces so much opposition that it explicitly must be 'Heard again, again, again' (line 371). But repetitiveness, however candidly confessed, is not necessarily justified. So, you should consider the various other defences that are implicitly advanced.

Least persuasive perhaps is the implied appeal to genre and a particular audience. Ballads do tend to accumulate force by redeploying the same rhetorical devices; as do political speeches aimed at a mass-audience. Certainly, the speech from lines 147 to the end of the poem does reiterate its point about the massive power latent in the sheer numbers of its audience: 'Ye are many – they are few' (lines 155, 376). But it is 'Ye' here (and in lines 165, 181, 187, 196, 295, 301, 302, 306, 323, 332) – never 'We'. The poet can appeal to, but not identify with, this audience for whom the simple ballad-style is adopted.

Yet, the poet here is far from being some superior intellect who can comfortably patronize the taste of those whom he addresses. The distance from which that isolatedly singular 'I' must speak in the opening stanza is confessed as an embarrassment. The poem does not claim to originate with the poet who 'lay asleep in Italy' but with 'a voice' reaching him 'from over the Sea' in England. And that voice leads him only half-way towards the folk-ballads of those ill-educated demonstrators whose voices cried out in pain or rage as the sabres struck at Peterloo.

Shelley's title, in evoking the literary-dramatic conventions of the court masque, means, of course, to expose the shabby theatrical fraud of those who currently prop up the English throne. Yet, the knowledge of such a form – admitted to by the poet and perhaps sought in his readers – may confess the uneasy gulf between the poem's own privileged origins and the deprivations (educational as well as physical) of those whose cause it seeks to serve.

The openly far more refined poet is led while he still sleeps into 'Visions of Poesy'. This elegant phrase is apt to the genre of dream-narrative which is evoked here: a genre associated with an ancient, courtly tradition in early English poetry: poetry that Shelley (and perhaps his poem's anticipated audience) does know; but poetry that is far less likely to have been met by the ordinary, working 'Men of England': the 'Ye' supposedly addressed from line 147 on. The dream-narrative convention of high literature customarily ends with the poet's awakening. The omission of this from 'The Mask of Anarchy' may discreetly maintain to the end of the poem that apologetic sense of being at an inadequate distance (culturally as well as topographically) with which the poem begins. More than once, we *are* asked to envisage that the 'Men of England' will wake up to injustice and to their responsibility for eliminating it – they will 'Rise . . . after slumber' (lines 151, 372). But the poet himself is never seen escaping his own slumber.

Yet, though it is as a somnambulist that he is 'led . . . / To walk' (lines 3–4), his 'Visions' do embrace a range of tone and topic that is disconcertingly wider than the soothingly narrow register of traditional dream-narrative Romances. Stanza 2, for instance begins with the same two words that initiate 'Ozymandias': 'I met'. But what confronts the speaker here is not some dreamily nondescript 'traveller' but the far blunter term of 'Murder', followed at once by the murderer's name.

Naming names is sometimes regarded as vulgar; and perhaps it is momentarily shocking to find 'Castlereagh' blundering, with coarsely prosaic specificity, into a scene where we had been promised only the 'Visions of Poesy'. But the indecorous disjunction of styles clearly has point. The elegant imprecisions of conventional 'Poesy' may, in other cases, keep us so high-mindedly concerned with timeless universals that we never look down to see what hideously specific crimes, in our own particular time and supposedly on our own behalf, government agencies are committing. The leap from what could be a harmlessly melodramatic generality of 'Murder' to the palpably real Foreign Secretary, and by association to the specifics of his lethal policies, is clumsily sudden. But it is an unmasking precisely designed to make readers, the habitual consumers of *verbal* art, blush at their gullibility.

The poem is arguably committed to demonstrating how words work ideologically. Words may seem to represent 'real things'. But in practice they are more often used to *mis*represent; since their actual function is not to describe 'reality' but to embody and enforce ideas. To expose this, the poem may commute between varying languages in which we talk ourselves into (or, potentially, out of) the 'slavery' identified in line 209. But some of these languages have such enormous, if unnoticed, power precisely because they themselves avoid – and implicitly prohibit – too much variation. And here, I think, we find a more adequate explanation of the poem's repetitiveness. For instance, the terminological conspiracy of line 37's 'GOD AND KING AND LAW' is repeated with only minor variations in lines 61, 69 and 71. Surely, this reiteration is necessary if we are to hear and understand the poem's point about the power of slogans, the capacity of repeated phrases to acquire mystifying associations.

Some of the stasis imposed on the reader in the first 85 lines of the poem is designed, I suspect, to reflect the apparently inescapable stagnation in which England is held by its conservative government's 'Anarchy'. There seems no prospect of change; and the *inter*changeability of those who have society in this stranglehold evokes at once both their strength and their sterility. Castlereagh is no different from Murder. Nor is he really distinguishable from Eldon and Fraud or from Sidmouth and Hypocrisy. All three (or six) are as bad as each other. Nor can they, without misrepresentation, be told apart from their lackeys: that drearily anonymous horde of 'Bishops, lawyers, peers or spies' (line 29). These in turn appropriately sound almost indistinguishable from all those servile supporters who are in fact their victims: that 'adoring multitude' which allows this élite to trample it under foot until it is no more than 'a mire of blood' (line 40).

All speak the same circular nonsense in which 'King' and 'God' and 'Lord' are interchangeably synonymous. In line 44, for instance, can you tell which totem-figure is meant by 'their Lord'? If we take the 'troop . . . Waving each a bloody sword' literally and specifically, then these cavalrymen at Peterloo may see themselves as in the 'service' of some general or magistrate or local peer. But they will obey such a figure as 'their Lord' because, in their language, he is the present representative of some absent but superior 'Lord': 'King' George or the Christian 'God', perhaps. But this 'King' is anyway supposedly no more (and no less) than the earthly representative of that same 'God'. And both – to those conservatives of the Church-and-State, Law-and-Order party – are embodied in the 'Law' that the King's tory ministers make. Anarchy can be reverenced equally in line 69 as either 'Law' or 'God'.

The poem refuses to give these figures distinctive character-ization so as to insist upon the monotonous suffering that they impose. All constitute the ubiquitous, unvarying reign of that 'Anarchy' which seems as eternally powerful as 'Death' itself 'in the Apocalypse' (line 32).

I think we are meant to be so steeped in resignation to this conspiracy's tedious power that at first we can scarcely recognise the fleeting form of 'Hope'. She scurries past muffled in a mere adverbial clause appended to a sentence that is already into its fifth line (line 86). We need to experience the difficulty, in the context of England under Anarchy, of registering even the possibility of hope. It is far easier to dismiss optimism as sheer lunacy – Hope seems 'a *Maniac* maid'; or mistake it for its opposite – 'she looked more like Despair' (lines 86–9).

This is a culture where the 'smooth' statesman, Castlereagh, actually means 'Murder' (lines 5–6); where the 'ermined gown' of the state's highest justice needs to be decoded as a penchant for knocking out the brains of little children (lines 15–21); and where to be 'Clothed . . . with light' from 'the Bible' is in fact to be shadowy as 'night' and vicious as 'a crocodile' (22–5). Here all that glitters most enticingly is certainly not gold; but merely the disguise of death. In line 66, the vaunted 'glory' of battles like Waterloo turns out to be composed of 'gold' and 'blood' which are virtually synonymous; and the magical paraphernalia of coronation – 'sceptre, crown, and globe,/ And the gold-inwoven robe' (lines 80–1) are merely the fancy dress that hides 'Anarchy, the Skeleton' (line 74): the mori-bund and yet murderous reality that lies behind all this high-sounding cant. Only Anarchy, through the mark on his brow like that of homicide's inventor, can truly say 'I AM GOD AND KING AND LAW' (line 37). The rest are only understudies, feebly imper-sonating this ultimate expert in 'Murder', 'Fraud' and 'Hypocrisy' (lines 5, 14 and 24). Readers, trying to read any truth 'In this ghastly

masquerade' (line 27), glimpse 'Hope' in line 86 so briefly that she
has virtually already 'fled past'. We learn what it feels like to fear that
Hope too may really have portended the very opposite of the name
that she carries.

The words that 'she cried out' do remain 'in the air' to be
recorded (line 89). But, words we have learnt, are not necessarily to
be trusted. Her despairing view of history is one of decline into
dotage (lines 90–3). All its earlier signs of hope have perished; and,
ultimately, she has nothing better to articulate, than a repeated wail
of 'Misery, o Misery!' (lines 94–7). She sounds like an incoherent
adolescent, jeering at her father and pitying herself. Such 'Hope' is
apparently doomed, unless aided by some other force, to die at this
very moment, beneath trampling hooves. These are at once both the
hideously specific realities of the Manchester soldiers' horses and the
vast web of thought and language which empowers the mighty forces
of 'Murder, Fraud and Anarchy' (lines 98–101).

The mere 'mist', at first so 'small . . . weak and frail' and
eventually no more than 'a Shape', that does come to her rescue is no
more than – but perhaps no less than – 'an image' (lines 103–10).
The poem will later argue that, were 'tyrants' to be challenged by an
adequate image of 'Freedom', they 'would flee/ Like a dream's dim
imagery' (lines 213–16).

Power for Shelley does, of course, derive from imagery, subjectively interpreted. It has little to do with concrete 'facts' that can be
objectively measured. The soldiers at Peterloo, for instance, might
objectively have been thought powerless since they were so vastly
outnumbered by the demonstrators. But they had on their side the
legitimizing symbolism of their uniforms: they are later explicitly
'Troops of armed *emblazonry*' (line 310). They were visibly associated, mounted as they were, with a class used to feeling superior,
looking down upon, and (at least metaphorically) riding rough-shod
over, the pedestrian protests of the lower orders. More importantly
perhaps the verbal weapons were on their side. An all-pervasive
rhetoric made them embody the full, intimidating weight of 'GOD
AND KING AND LAW'. An imagery that both sides conspired to
interpret as potent nerved the soldiers to charge and kill just as it
intimidated the demonstrators into flight and into *being* killed.

So, the 'Shape' that can answer adequately to such power, is
appropriately built up out of figurative signs. The accumulating
metaphors and similes of the portrait in lines 110–24 may, illumi-
natingly enough, remind you of the 'Hymn's' description of 'Intellectual Beauty'. After all, this Shape also lacks any stable, concrete
existence. It too arrives and departs 'so fast' that though its 'presence'
is felt, any attempt to see it discovers only 'empty air' (lines 119–
21). It too is essentially 'Intelletual' in that it is registered by 'the
heads of men' and the seeds it sows spring up exclusively as

'Thoughts' (lines 119 and 125). This new, reinforced image of Hope transforms her from the 'Maniac Maid' who lay down helplessly on the ground. The 'multitude' (still imitatively as 'prostrate' as she herself had been earlier) are now equipped to look up and see her as a 'maiden most serene'. Thanks to the intervention of the mysterious 'Shape', Hope can now be understood as a figure of stately but all-conquering resolution. Her dignified 'walking' can be imagined as a progress that destroys 'Anarchy' and banishes the 'Horse of Death' on which he has ridden; though not before its hoofs have demolished all the human agents of its murderous regime (lines 126–34).

These lines might seem a suitable point for an earlier conclusion. Is this not our happy ending? What more is there to say? Well, the poem insists that there *is* a great deal more which does need precisely to be *said*: a direct speech is signalled as beginning at line 147; and it runs to the last line, thus constituting well over half the poem. To find out whether this massive speech is a pointful addition, we might ask: Who is the speaker?

DISCUSSION

In some sense, of course, these lines are, like the entire poem, spoken by the figure of the poet: the 'I' of lines 1 and 5. It is he who has been telling us, from line 5 onwards, what he remembers having seen and heard in his dream. And the fact that he is only dreaming is one explanation of why the end of Anarchy and its gang at line 134 cannot give the poem any persuasive happy ending. The poet's dream at this point may have become far less of a nightmare for him. But outside the private cinema of his fantastical unconsciousness, the real world in which the English people suffer has not altered.

The poem may therefore carry on after line 134 so as to confess that the poet's own personal hope, his ability to dream privately of a moment when reform has been achieved, is useless on its own. A more literary version of this explanation might focus on the dream-narrative that governs lines 1–134 and the arguably contrasting genre of popular song or political speech which operates more obtrusively from lines 147 to the end. To have effect on England in 1819, the poet may need to abandon traditional forms and an elite readership, acquiring instead a new voice in which to reach a new audience.

But is such a voice available; and, if so, where is it likely to be found? Lines 135–47 are tentative about the identity of the speaker that is about to be introduced. The dreaming poet seems to withdraw, no longer able to claim that he himself heard this new voice. It merely '*Was* heard and felt'. Its 'words of joy and fear' seem almost to have created themselves. Instead of passively having been spoken, they actively 'arose' (lines 137–8). Admittedly, the 'indignant Earth', stained with her children's blood, is introduced as an outraged mother-figure; but the poem reiterates that it is only 'As if' the ensuing speech originates in her (lines 139 and 147).

The fact that the rest of the poem *is* speech, directly addressed in vocatives to the ordinary, working 'Men of England', seems more important than any guess the poet can yet make as to who or what will find the words to make that audience 'Rise like Lions'. For the time being, the people exist unrecorded and inarticulate within an essentially '*unwritten* story' (line 149). The folk ballad that Shelley's verse-form here imitates may have given them some way of telling their own tales; but that is an innately oral tradition rather than a written one; and it has too seldom been politicized. Literature, being arguably the propaganda of some victorious minority after its struggle for power against some equally unrepresentative clique of the élite, has hitherto excluded the majority. Yet the control and use of words is crucial if, in actuality rather than dream, the people are ever to gain their freedom.

The Shape supplied 'Thoughts' (line 125); but not words, apparently. 'Hope', was helped into abandoning her self-defeating 'maniac' babble of 'Misery o Misery' (lines 86, 97); but she was not then equipped with any new voice. It is in an absolute silence that she supposedly rallies 'the prostrate multitude' and defeats Anarchy. Perhaps this change without words strains our credulity even more than most elements in the dream. It has, after all, been the power of Anarchy's own words – signalled by direct speech marks in lines 37, 61–9 and 71–3 – that originally reduced this 'multitude' to 'adoring', 'prostrate' helplessness (lines 41 and 126).

The speech from line 147 to the end is thus partly justified as a long-delayed lesson in language. The crucial word to understand and use – 'Freedom' – is put on the top of the agenda: 'What is Freedom?' (line 156); but, for an audience that has no experience of such a concept, the answer must wait until appeal has been made to what they already do know – 'slavery'; and the next fifteen stanzas are devoted to a painstaking definition of that word (lines 156–212). These may begin by saying that the audience already 'can tell' what slavery is only 'too well'; but what is meant here is only that through bitterly familiar experience they can *feel* what the *state* of slavery is like. They have not yet learnt enough about the use of 'slavery' as a *word* and the ways in which it can allow them literally 'to tell' the tale of their present humiliation with a voice that will end it. It can, according to lines 158–9, in fact be used as the 'very name' for their own condition in England (rather than just that of Africans forcibly transported to the distant Americas). And, in this 'slavery', the English people have been reduced by those who exploit them to synonymity with other terms too: the mere tools of their trade, for instance (lines 164–7).

The definition of 'slavery' expands to include manifestations as superficially various and as ubiquitous as that of 'Anarchy', its partner in this sick symbiosis. The psychic subjugation which makes each worker a prideless 'slave *in soul*' provokes oppression to more and more outlandish abuses of power until a sudden rage for 'revenge' could make the victim of 'slavery' indistinguishable from the anarchists who impose it: an 'exchange' of 'blood for blood, and wrong for wrong' in which no actual change in society can be achieved (lines 184–95).

Against any such resort to violence, line 196 offers an explicit prohibition: 'Do not thus when ye are strong'. But the very next lines (197–212) return to expounding the full, degrading definition of 'slavery'. They eventually insist that neither 'wild beasts' nor 'savage men' would so gutlessly endure such abasement; and indeed that such supposedly inferior species have never been tested by this scale of insult (lines 209–12). The poem here surely goads its audience to an uprising that is unlikely to be non-violent. And indeed the summons to 'Rise like Lions' (animals not associated with pacifism) has been offered earlier and will be repeated at the end (lines 151 and 372).

How far do you think the proposal of 'a great Assembly' (lines 266–306) or the recommendation of passive resistance (lines 307–51) bridges (or even exacerbates) this apparent inconsistency?

What seems certain is that the language-lesson is not being taught by the poet in his own patronising person, as one who claims to be clear where the audience are still in the dark. Some degree of muddle and hesitation is in the voice making the speech. And that too is one explanation of the speech's (and the overall poem's) length. Equivocation between more than one point of view inevitably takes more time than a single, unambivalent appeal.

Consider, as perhaps the key-example, the issue of words and their power. There is implicit hesitation about what verbal register is appropriate to this speech and its audience: an audience that may be the workers themselves; or the liberal-minded amongst Shelley's own cultural peers. For example, what a labourer might think of as France is called 'Gaul' (line 245): familiar to those whose superior education had required translation of Latin texts. The service-issue swords of the British cavalry work through a series of brutally simple monosyllables as they 'Slash and stab and maim and hew' (line 346). Yet they are also 'scimitars . . . like sphereless stars' (lines 319–20).

Does the familiarity of simple nouns like 'clothes and fire and wood' (line 225) make the remnants of a more elegant vocabulary seem even more intrusive? Would those who, through poverty, are compelled to think in such concrete terms accept the proposed connections with abstracts such as 'Justice' (line 234), 'Wisdom' (line 238) and 'Peace' (line 242)? Or do the latter still evoke a more patrician discourse?

There is also far more explicit ambivalence as to whether *any* words that could have sufficient power can be found. If only the workers themselves 'could . . . answer' the question of 'What art thou, Freedom', then 'tyrants would flee' (lines 213–15). But is that adequate answer likely to be verbal? At one point, the prayer is: 'let deeds' – and explicitly '*not* words' – demonstrate Freedom's 'exceeding loveliness' (line 265). Yet, at an earlier point, the audience have been told they must use 'measured words' to 'Declare' explicitly their God-given rights; and that their own 'strong and simple words' are reliably 'Keen' weapons and secure shields (lines 301–6). The aim is later to be 'Eloquent, oracular'; but the demonstrators who are to create this high-sounding 'inspiration' are to do so, not through making speeches, but through surrendering to 'slaughter' (lines 364–7).

The very next lines, however, predict that 'these words' will become an irresistibly potent mantra, spelling out 'oppression's doom' (lines 368–71). Which lines do you take '*these* words' to describe? Is it the whole poem which has suddenly become so immodest as to claim such future force? Or is there the humbler implication lurking in 'then' (line 368) that it will only be if and when the people act with crushing courage that 'these words' gain significance?

The third alternative – and the one I favour – is that the phrase refers far more narrowly, pointing forward only to the next stanza. Perhaps this disturbed and disturbing poem ends confident only in 'these words' that constitute its last five lines. These are indeed magnificently memorable. Their rousing summons, which may sound appropriately spontaneous, has in fact been carefully wrought. Notice, for instance, how the only polysyllable, 'unvanquishable', is launched by the sturdy monosyllables around it into sounding as massive and irresistible as its meaning.

Elsewhere, 'The Mask of Anarchy' is often more embarrassed, as the work of the wrong poet in the wrong place at the wrong time: at risk of being left speechless with outrage at the news carried by that 'voice from over the sea'; aware that his own, most highly cultured voice would not be appropriate; and yet wrestling with stamina and agility through a sequence of attempts at finding a style that can do justice to the appalling *in*justice being suffered by those for whom he cares but with whom he can never feel at ease. You could see the entire poem as establishing a context which will empower the last five lines. For nearly 150 lines, the poem searches for a voice in which to address directly the 'Men of England'. It then, in lines 151–5, offers the five lines that it will repeat at the end. By the time that we read them again as the poem's conclusion, the intervening material surely has given them enormously greater impact. The poem's length seems to me justifiable as an essential part of its meaning.

Shelley's variety is such that our next poem, which is no more than a sonnet, arguably uses the very brevity of its form to convey its more decisive account of the political situation. Please turn to 'England in 1819' (Webb, p. 90). This time, read the poem aloud, trying to notice – and to evaluate – its use of sound. Consider, for instance, the more obvious examples of alliteration. What is their effect? And think, too, about syntax. What do shape and length of sentence require of the speaking voice? How do these affect the tone?

DISCUSSION

I find the first line an exhilarating shock. Before we can reach the potentially resounding title of 'King', its pretensions are demolished by no less than five epithets: three, crushingly simple monosyllables – 'old, mad, blind'; then the more expansive 'despised, and dying'. The pace with which these follow each other might suggest a tone of spitting fury. But their precision may recommend a voice closer to icily controlled scorn. George III was indeed at the time in his eighties. He had, for many years been regarded, even by devout royalists, as incurably insane. He was also within a few months of his death. Throughout all five adjectives, the thumping repetition of the '*d*' drums out, unifying the onslaught. Yet, as the '*d*' subtly shifts from the ends to the beginnings of words, we can hear the poem already preparing to release this almost pathetic, spent force and to focus its attack on those who do rule in Regency England.

The princes being called 'blind in blood' may seem too easy an alliterative trick (line 6). But both words could have more than enough meaning to justify it. In a society where power is essentially inherited, all that may be passed on down the bloodline may be a disability in which sons, like their fathers, 'neither see nor feel nor know' (line 4). More obviously, we have been invited to think of the aristocracy as leeches, attached to the sick country as if to cure, but in fact bleeding it dry. (Leeches, literally blind to the bodies they drain, were used in contemporary medicine solely to suck blood.) Moreover, there may be some anticipation of the next line's allusion to Peterloo where the soldiers were perhaps acting in blind fury, 'Drunk . . . with intoxication' of the very blood they were shedding as 'The Mask of Anarchy' puts it (lines 48–9).

What of the comparably obtrusive alliteration offered in 'starved and stabbed' (line 7)? Clearly, the repeated 'st' hints at the stammering staccato of a voice almost incoherent with indignation. But the revelation of Peterloo was precisely that the long-standing economic oppression would, if challenged, be maintained by legal murder: that the concepts of 'starved and stabbed' would prove as shockingly interdependent as they sound here. The poem also contrives, through 'untilled', to remind us of the unemployment produced when landlords decided that profits did not justify full use of their estates. The supposedly 'natural' laws of supply and demand which produced agricultural recession led to decisions as conscious and as lethal as that of the magistrates who ordered the cavalry-charge. Without wages many families did die of malnutrition. They, Shelley's alliterative phrase suggests, are not to be separated from those cut down at Peterloo.

Perhaps the poem's most effective use of sound is the patiently accumulative syntax: the sequence of adjectives, nouns and adjectival clauses which the reading voice must assemble before reaching, in the penultimate line of this single-sentence poem, its main verb. There may be hints of a cheering capacity to self-destruct in the leeches image for the ruling class; or in their 'two-edged' army (lines 8–9). But surely the overall tendency of the first 12 lines is towards weary despair? Nouns and adjectives keep us waiting so long that we begin to wonder whether a main verb, a word that could promise significant action, will ever be admitted. Most of the subsidiary verbs are *past* participles, suggesting that what has been must always be. Some of these are negatives forbidding us to credit the activity that they evoke: 'untilled', 'unrepealed'. The most verbally alive forces in the first 12 lines are those wealth-protecting and blood-thirsty 'laws' which, aided by the temptations of agents provocateurs, do effectively both 'tempt and slay'. These sound all too active in the present.

Elsewhere the grammar evokes only stagnation: until, strikingly positioned at the beginning of line 13, the main verb suddenly appears. This in two adjacent, decisively stressed syllables buries all the previously described powers. As if by definition, all 'Are graves'. The apparently forceful leaders and institutions turn out, after all, to be even now as moribund as that 'dying King' whom they represent.

The sentence's long-postponed main verb compresses the whole, preceding description of contemporary England into a single noun, 'graves'. This acts like a tightly coiled spring, 'from which' the poem's last adjectival clause can suddenly release all the energy of an optimistic hypothesis. The prospect of a dazzling transformation allows that startlingly dynamic verb 'Burst' to explode at the beginning of the last line.

But what of the *end* of that line and of the poem? The final word, through rhyme, recalls that this glorious eruption is by no means certain: it only '*may* . . . illumine our tempestuous day'. The poem thus closes less confident in its forecast than in its bitter observations about the present. Yet 'our . . . day' being allowed the last word could turn the tentativeness of 'may' into an invitation to accept what is 'our' responsibility. What can only be hypothesized, not promised, may amount to a stimulating demand. The tempest need not be that of an oppression which is allowed to rage on. It could be made our own stormy efforts to struggle for a glorious future.

Ambiguities about the import of tempestuous weather, and the possibility that apparent death may presage glorious rebirth, are central too in 'Ode to the West Wind'. But, though the poem was written at much the same time as 'The Mask of Anarchy' and 'England in 1819', it makes no explicit reference to specific, contemporary, events such as Peterloo. Indeed, is it so much more interested in poetry (or, more precisely, in the poet's own experience of his role and responsibilities) that it is scarcely a political poem at all? Try to make up your own mind about this issue before considering my view. Please read the poem now. Here too, the more you can register sound-effects and sentence-shape, the closer you should get to the poem's meaning.

DISCUSSION

I take the 'Ode' to be, not only a poem *about* the desirability of movement, but one whose own chronology of clearly defined movements is essential to its meaning. So I am arranging my comments in sequence, stanza by stanza.

1 (lines 1–14)
The cumulative alliteration of the opening vocative phrase makes the 'wild West Wind' sound invigorating. So, the more sinister and morbid elements of the ensuing lines may come as a jarring surprise. The inversion of 'leaves dead' insists on fatality by posing 'dead' as the rhyme-word at the end of the line. The sentence, however, hurtles on, driving these seemingly finished 'dead' to live again as 'ghosts'. They flee like mobs panicked by plague. The context might force one to visualize (uncomfortably) 'Yellow' as the ugly hue of 'pestilence-stricken' skin; and '*hectic* red', though evoking the pace of the poem itself, could also highlight the pace of death brought to the multitudes. The contradictions in 'black, and pale' might resolve themselves as the darkly funereal yoked to the pallidly dying.

Yet the baldly exposed 'corpse within its grave' – there are no qualifying adjectives to dress it – is juxtaposed with the lyrically literary 'azure sister of the Spring' whose 'living hues' could seem an absolute contrast to the death-evoking colours of line 4.

Opposing moods and different conventions of language seem to be in potentially dizzying collision. At this stage of the poem, I think we are meant to be aware of paradox, to sense dichotomies, to glimpse the possibility that this wild wind could be more than its literal self; and yet to feel so swept up in its unceasing energy that its meaning must be sought later. Its unfailing dynamism, which lurches us so rapidly from the morbid to the vivacious, is embodied in a 14-line stanza which remains a single, ever-elaborating vocative until its last three words. Only then does the grammar shift from invocation (with all the supporting adjectival clauses that describe the invoked) to imperative.

Superficially, this imperative is obviously an appeal to the wind, so lengthily described in the previous 13 lines. But, at some level, it is surely the poem's reader who is insistently told to 'hear, O hear!'. I am not suggesting that the first stanza is a mere drum-roll to make us prick up our ears and start thinking in time for later stanzas. Stanza 1 itself must already have offered some hints as to what significance, whether political or otherwise, the wind is to have. But I suspect these are inseparable from its task of inviting us to become adequately energetic readers, willing to contribute creatively to the poem's search for meaning. As an example, please consider the demands implied by the enigmatic imagery of line 11. What sense – or senses – can you make from the offered similarity of 'buds' to 'flocks'; and how can either 'feed in air'?

We can see buds as being stirred into wind-shaken blossoms which flutter off like flocks of birds. Flying birds can seem to be eating mere air because they feed on insect-life invisible to the human eye. Their nourishment thus represents one 'unseen presence' (line 2) of an ecosystem that is indeed both 'Destroyer and Preserver'. Alternatively, the buds may blossom into flocks of sheep. These could seem to 'feed in air' because, with Spring's warmer weather summoning them higher and higher up the mountain-side, they dwindle to speck-like forms. Perhaps they are silhouetted on the topmost ridge that forms the sky-line and appear to seek sustenance from the sky itself. This force which, in Spring, with the benign protectiveness of a shepherd, will be 'driving . . . flocks to feed' is the same force of the cycling seasons as appears in Autumn: by whose breath, the dead leaves 'Are driven' to helpless flight (line 3). That one verb of motion – to drive – moves us to see sustaining aspiration in one context, forlorn impotence in the other. It thus invites us to discover the dynamic emotiveness of a force which is 'moving everywhere' (line 13).

Am I being too industriously fanciful in trying to make the 'flocks' not only birds but sheep? The route from buds to blossoms, whose whiteness in turn suggests sheep, is perhaps tortuous. Light colouring may be the key connection here; but has its significance been confusingly reversed since we were asked to associate things that looked 'pale' with 'ghosts' and 'pestilence' (lines 3–5)? Connections so elusively compressed and transformations so rapidly achieved do make great demands on the reader. But the poem, in praying for union with the wind, may also be seeking new kinds of co-operation between a more fluid text and a more actively participating reader.

2 (lines 15–28)

Here, the poem's topography is even more challenging and fluid. The sky's 'clouds' are explicitly 'like Earth's decaying leaves' (line 2). They thus recall the landscape of the previous stanza. Yet they are 'Shook from the tangled boughs' of both 'Heaven *and Ocean*' (line 3) – an ocean which, in a more literal form, will be the setting of the next stanza.

The clouds are also like 'Angels' (line 4) – perhaps in the precise sense of messengers. They herald 'rain and lightning' whose fertilizing, illuminating power guarantees change. Do I import too much from other Shelley poems (such as 'England in 1819') in finding, as early as here, an invitation to hear the wind as an 'approaching storm' which will bring *political* change? But, in this stanza, the Ode's emphasis – however we choose to apply it – is indisputably on turbulent energies born out of an apparently moribund inertia. The wind is at once 'dirge/ Of the dying year' (lines 23–4); and a prophet of tumult whose prediction is decisive: 'Black rain, and fire, and hail', in two confidently stressed monosyllables, 'will burst' (line 28). The 'vast sepulchre' is not only the burial-ground of the past; it is also the pregnantly 'congregated might' of the future (lines 25–6).

3 (lines 29–42)

Are the swirling cross-currents of rhythm, the rippling evocations of half-formed meanings, exhilarating in their mobility or just frustratingly opaque? And does the syntax (appropriately as unstable as the wind-swept ocean) produce stimulating or merely tiresome puzzles? What, for example, do you take the subject of 'saw', in line 33, to be?

One answer would be the Mediterranean (introspectively contemplating its own depths). This would continue the syntactical movement initiated in line 30: 'he lay . . . And saw'. An alternative candidate is the West Wind itself. We would then pick up the verb of line 29, and read 'Thou . . . didst waken . . . And saw'.

Whoever saw the underwater city, it is itself equivocal. Is it a real city: whether on the ocean floor, or reflected from its position on the coast? Or is it only an optical illusion: a creative interpretation of the billowing seaweed; or of the glimmering sky reflected on the heaving surface? Such illusions would be the product of the wind. Its pressure would 'waken' the appearance of a city 'Quivering within the wave'.

But the wind, summoned by the poem partly as its Muse, is in one of its key-roles 'Creator': an ideal model for the human writer to imitate. So, how acceptable, in the context of this verbal artefact, are my loaded terms of 'real' and 'illusion'. Even if the city does only *seem* to be there, is it any less significant to the poem's articulation of creatively swirling energy, its celebration of a power that can conjure vibrant life out of apparently sterile materials? Perhaps the stanza, far from inviting us to produce dogmatic answers to the questions that it begs, aims to ween us from our dependence on rigidly exclusive distinctions; to teach us the wisdom of uncertainty; with which we might nerve ourselves to seek the change whose precise results none can predict.

4 *(lines 43–56)*
Please look at stanza 4 again, noting particularly its use of pronouns, and try to decide how far it represents a significant deviation from the pattern established by the previous three stanzas.

DISCUSSION

Even in its opening phrase, stanza 4 surely does announce a quite new stance and tone. Instead of 'O . . . wind' (stanza 1), or 'Thou' (stanzas 2 and 3), the focus is now, not on the object of the speech's address, but on the subjective speaker: 'If I . . .'.

Hitherto the poem has tried to sound almost anonymous, so absorbed in the forces it invokes as to lose its authorship in identification with a wind powerful enough to hurl earth, sea and sky into the melting-pot of its imagery. This suppression of personality, which has perhaps already sounded precarious, now disintegrates. The subjectivity that comes into play here foregrounds the figure of the poet; and what he discusses is himself. The first-person pronoun – varying through 'I', 'me', 'my' – appears nine times within fourteen lines. Is the new stance narrowingly self-centred and even self-pitying? Or does the poet dramatize his own situation by carefully controlled use of the earlier sections in which it has been the dazzlingly accomplished wind that plays theatrical games on a world-scale stage?

Certainly, the longing to respond as 'leaf', 'cloud' and 'wave' (lines 43–5 and 53) must recall the sequence of settings in stanzas 1, 2 and 3. Moreover, each of these earlier stanzas has, in its alternation between vocative description and prayer, implied that the poem means to portray, not only the wind, but also the supplicant who needs its support.

Yet the past which is mourned here does not seem to me just the private idyll of one particular childhood. The conditional clauses of the stanza's opening lines surely insist upon the fact that the poet, unable to be 'leaf' or 'cloud' or 'wave' belongs to *homo sapiens*, is compelled to be part of its history: with the greater hopes and greater disappointments which that involves. The 'boyhood' coincided with a phase of widely-shared optimism about the chance of radical transformation for European societies. It made the poet a 'comrade' of all that seemed most dynamic in the natural world. It allowed him, like so many others at that time, to glimpse 'a vision' of humanity as actually surpassing the most inspiring models of freedom and energy amongst other earthly forces (lines 48–51). The 'heavy weight of hours' is surely not just the poet's own advancing age (Shelley, after all, was just 27 at the time of composition). The passing years that had metaphorically 'chained and bowed' the voice of hope had all too literally imprisoned and humiliated those who fought for freedom. Across Europe, reactionary governments seemed to have demonstrated that, though the West Wind might be the great 'Uncontrollable' who is innately 'tameless', its libertarian, human imitators could be tamed easily enough.

This taming, at its most crushingly effective, reduced each potential 'comrade' to seeing himself as an isolated subjectivity and his opponents, not as politicians who could be sacked, but as the innate, unalterable, natural facts of human existence: 'the thorns of life' itself, on which each lonely ego is doomed to 'fall' and 'bleed' (line 54).

Stanza 4 is the first which does not end in the command or plea of 'hear!'. Is the poet now so much more confident that he has the attention of his audience? Surely not. The likelier implication is that memories of a former vigour, which now seems to be lost, distract him into talking more to himself, and less to the forces of the future.

5 (lines 57–70)

Please consider two questions here. Firstly, is the subject now more obviously poetry (or even this 'Ode' itself)? Secondly, though first-person pronouns are frequent here too, are there senses in which this stanza achieves (or at least audibly attempts) a less narrowly personal tone?

DISCUSSION

The opening plea to be used as the wind's 'lyre' (a traditional symbol of poetry, whether specifically lyrical or not) is surely more precise in its implications than the previous stanzas' hope of being 'lift[ed] as a wave, a leaf, a cloud' (line 54). The wind itself, with its 'harmonies' (line 59), is now more obviously a creative artist whose medium is sound; and it can make use of the poet. It can, 'from both' the literal forest's Autumn *and* the poet's own identification with the 'leaves . . . falling', derive 'a deep . . . tone' (lines 57–60). The text's own 'words' (line 67) have not been explicitly mentioned in earlier stanzas. Implicitly, they have been associated with earth, air and water. But they now openly aspire to the fourth element of fire. The Promethean image specifies the fiery power of 'words *among mankind*'. Is this a generalized claim that poetry can change minds? Or is it more disconcertingly specific in pleading for itself, recommending 'the incantation of this' (particular) 'verse' (line 65)?

Perhaps this is a false choice. The first-person pronouns here are more positively linked to those second-person pronouns that invoke the larger forces to which the poem addresses itself. Consider the immediate juxtapositions of 'me thy' (line 57) or 'thou me' (line 62). This surely signals a restored confidence, if not in the poet's own abilities, at least in his capacity to communicate with – and draw strength from – the Wind. The possessive 'my' – which appears five times in the stanza – can sound self-possessed; unlike the 'I' that appeared six times in the previous stanza and sometimes risked sounding merely self-conscious.

Perhaps the poem accepts that it is, for the present, doomed to think and speak in personalized terms; but finds a way of dedicating such terminology to the more communal values which a transformed future would allow. Stanza 4 had articulated the self as essentially singular: '*a* . . . leaf', '*a* . . . cloud', '*A* wave', '*a* wave, *a* leaf, *a* cloud', '*One* too like thee' (lines 43–5, 53, 56). There, the sense of personality as vulnerably individualized led to self-doubt, the fear that what once felt 'tameless, and swift, and proud' might now stay 'chained and bowed'. By contrast, in stanza 5, the recovery of freedom and pride is sought through a redefinition of the self in terms of plurals: 'my . . . thoughts', 'my . . . words'. Such expressions adapt the poet's mind and writings to fit the *mass* movement to which they now contribute. The poet's own, plural 'leaves' merge with those of an entire forest (line 58); and 'Will' become components in a whole 'tumult . . . of mighty harmonies' (lines 59–60).

That momentarily confident use of the future tense in 'Will' reminds us that the Ode, like so much of Shelley's verse, is indeed 'prophecy' (line 69). The subject of its thought and the object of its address are the winds of change. These can turn each seed which now lies 'cold and low' in the 'grave' of its 'dark wintry bed' (lines 6–8) into 'a new birth' (line 64).

Yet the Ode admits that what, in the Europe of 1819, confronts it is still 'unawakened Earth'. This last, potentially dispiriting, phrase may be the end of a line; but it is not the end of the sentence. The beginning of the next line invites us to read on, looking beyond the present stupor of humanity, to the rousing 'trumpet of a prophecy'. Syntactical sequence also matters in the poem's final sentence, where present 'Winter' is indeed followed by future 'Spring'.

That future, of course, rests in the hands of people who, at the time of the poem's composition, are yet unborn. The poem longs to 'Scatter' its 'words' among distant generations of 'mankind'. What may seem no more than 'withered leaves' (a pun on the pages of a book, perhaps) will, through later 'incantation of this verse', be read as fertile seeds planted 'to quicken' that 'new birth' (line 64). Over a century and a half later, you may now be able to hear in such imagery associations which the poet of 1819 could not have specifically anticipated. You might, for instance, think of radio and television's power to disseminate 'thoughts' and 'words among mankind' since the term 'broadcasting' does, of course, derive from the sower's scattering of seed.

Should we try to suppress such ideas as anachronistic? Or should we accept the poem's own invitation to drive what might otherwise seem 'dead thoughts' into the energy of 'a new birth' (lines 64–5); to stir the 'ashes' of the Ode's past into the 'sparks' of our future (line 67)? The 'prophecy' here is not a restrictingly specific blueprint. The question asked in the Ode's last sentence is indeed a demanding one. It must be redefined by each generation's experience and answered by each new reader's frames of reference.

In that sense, the Ode does seem to me a political poem. Perhaps because of, rather than in spite of, its reluctance to make any precise references to contemporary politics, it is surely a resource now. The turbulent energies to which the poem appeals, the strenuous optimisms it recommends as needed all the more in freedom's darkest days, are a challenge still.

I have tried to show in this chapter the interdependence, for Shelley, of politics and poetry. Even in poems that focus on specific, topical events, Shelley is concerned with politics in a larger definition: one that requires the poet to be curious about the contribution that his own craft can make to the initiation of change. Conversely, less obviously topical lyrics, even where they most seem to be self-regarding artefacts, are still addressing themselves to the politics of England in 1819. Poems like the Ode do indeed ask us to think about poetry itself: about the various ways in which it can guide us to image the natural world; or to understand the poet's own past life; or to interpret his professional obligations to the future. Such imagery, far from being *merely* poetic, matters precisely *because* it tells us about poetry and its power. For Shelley, that power can transform human minds and eventually create a new society. And, in such a society, the institutions responsible for the Peterloo massacre would be literally unthinkable.

6. *Prometheus Unbound*

Shelley argued in his essay 'On Life':

> The difference is merely nominal between the two classes of thought,
> which are vulgarly distinguished by the names of ideas and of external
> objects.[1]

Prometheus Unbound is about 'ideas'. Shelley's sub-title may call it
'A Lyrical *Drama*'; but, in Act I at least, all the various named figures
to whom the speeches and songs are allocated can be interpreted as
different aspects of the hero's own thought-processes. Yet the world
that Prometheus thinks about is often recognizably the Europe of
1819. So, the poem may still be about 'external objects': repressive
institutions whose power might strike contemporary readers as all
too real; and events that, far from being imaginary, had been seen to
defeat the noblest of ideas. As Shelley gloomily observed:

> the mighty advantages of the French Revolution have been almost
> completely compensated by a succession of tyrants (for demagogues,
> oligarchies, usurpers and legitimate Kings are merely varieties of the
> same class) from Robespierre to Louis XVIII.[2]

We must have that dreary 'succession' of literal 'tyrants' in mind as
we read Shelley's allegorical drama of Titans and gods.

However, the poem is concerned, too, with the entire 'class'
of rulers: to classify that language of power in which the individual
'usurpers and legitimate Kings' of recent history have been 'merely
varieties'. So, we should not expect realistic, idiosyncratic
'characters'.

Prometheus Unbound is also poem rather than play in its lack of
any conventionally developing plot. The various voices may reflect
the hero's own shifting views of his situation; but that situation itself
remains, for most of the play, apparently unchanged. Prometheus'
immobility, helplessly chained to the rock, can be seen as an image of
his own moral, psychological and political inertia. Or, it may
symbolize those more literal bonds that the reactionary regimes of

post-Waterloo Europe imposed on anyone who fought for human rights. In either case, conventionally dynamic 'plot' would not just be inappropriate. Like naturalistic characterisation, it would actively contradict the poem's chosen agenda.

The heroine, Asia, is admittedly more mobile than the hero; and her actions do eventually lead, in Shelley's defiant rewriting of Aeschylus' more pessimistic story, to Prometheus' liberation. But it is again the attitudes which Asia symbolizes that matter most. Through Act I, where she does not appear, we begin to guess her significance, not only from what other voices say of her, but also through the presence of her two sisters. One of these, Ione, perhaps represents 'Memory': the ability to recall more inspiringly liberated moments of past history which may make the repressive present endurable. Asia's other sister, Panthea, can, as her name suggests, be associated with the notion of the earth as itself a divine unity needing no external creator; but she also represents Hope. You should notice that the opening stage-direction insists upon a non-European setting for the drama, and think about the relationship between the heroine's name and the literal Asia in which the action takes place.

Other voices tempt Prometheus either to resign himself to despair or to indulge in bitter hatred towards his enemy, Jupiter. Though Jupiter himself never appears, his significance is perhaps the most crucial issue that you should consider in reading the play. Is he a mere phantom created in the hero's own distraught mind? Or does he represent regimes that had all too real an existence in contemporary Europe? Remember Shelley's view that the difference between 'ideas' and 'external objects' is merely 'nominal'; but consider too that the nominal – the words in which we name our experiences – may be vital, not only to the play's medium, but also to its message.

Please now read Act I Scene i (Webb, pp. 33–56). Then turn back to read again the opening speech (lines 1–74, Webb, 33–5), before considering my comments below.

DISCUSSION

In 1820, when Act I was first published, Jupiter, as 'cruel King' (line 50) or 'great King' (line 457), would have suggested, not the merely symbolic side-show of twentieth-century monarchies, but the actualities of political power. George IV was King of England. His power, even when he had been only the Prince Regent, was such that the mildest criticism of him in print had landed authors like Leigh Hunt in gaol. It had been George's right to decide whether subversive labourers, like those who led the 1817 Pentridge uprising, should, after their public hanging, also be hacked into four quarters.[3]

Jupiter's regality associates him also with the Christian theology that supported monarchs. He is '*Heaven's* fell King' (line 140), 'the

Supreme Tyrant' (line 208) and – in a bold subversion of Christian prayer – '*our almighty* Tyrant' (line 161). Modern Christian worship, the poem argues, is thus like any other primitive superstition since religions have always been used as rationales for social injustice. The opening words call Jupiter 'Monarch of Gods and Daemons'. Through 'three thousand years' of so-called civilization (line 12), his 'ill tyranny' has embraced the most obvious cruelties of ancient religion (the piled corpses of men and women sacrificed to appease each primitive god); and those subtler 'hecatombs' of modern society which are composed of 'broken hearts'. I take this last phrase to mean the smashed psyches of those who have allowed themselves to be blackmailed – by lies about the threat of Hell or the promise of Heaven – into 'fear and self-contempt and barren hope' (lines 7–8). Every institutional religion is seen as having extorted the same 'knee-worship, prayer and praise,/ And toil' (lines 6–7).

But might these last terms list the typical demands of a *political*, rather than a religious institution? A royal court, for instance, thrives on grovelling petitioners; and a staggeringly extravagant one, like the Prince Regent's, had certainly required the 'toil' of 'multitudinous . . . slaves' amongst the working-class to fund it (lines 5 and 7). The alternative applicabilities of such terms neatly evoke the two-faced force of Jupiter. His power depends on reverence for both priests and political bosses. These equally claim a divine right to rule: one supposedly granted by 'Mighty God!/ Almighty' (lines 17–18).

Jupiter represents what Shelley elsewhere calls 'the philosophy of slavery and superstition', in which we kneel to gods and kings, accepting rules which 'we should in no manner be bound to obey, unless some dreadful punishment were attached to disobedience'. Genuinely benevolent morality cannot be motivated by either 'the anticipation of hellish agonies or the hope of heavenly reward'. Truly good acts, Shelley argues, are performed, not when one feels '*bound* or *obliged*', but 'willing'.[4] Prometheus cannot be unbound so long as his thoughts are chained to Jupiter's system of reward and punishment. A curse, in which he prays that 'hellish agonies' should merely be transferred from himself to his enemy, does nothing to weaken the mental structures that enslave. It just reinforces the assumption that power must always be a matter of intimidation or bribery, either bullying its victims into 'fear and self-contempt' or gulling them into 'barren hope'.

How far does Prometheus sound as if he has already begun to liberate himself? How often does he, by contrast, still seem bound to a rhetoric of threat? Please now consider the ambiguities in lines 9–11.

> Whilst me, who am thy foe, eyeless in hate,
> Hast thou made reign and triumph to thy scorn,
> O'er mine own misery and thy vain revenge.

DISCUSSION

The first-person pronoun, 'me', is accusative in anticipation of the speaker's role as object of the verb 'made' in the next line. Prometheus thus casts himself as the object of another's power, defines himself as no more than what he has been 'made' by Jupiter.

Yet between 'me' and the verb which governs it, that adjectival clause, 'who am thy foe', intervenes. Here, Prometheus strives to describe himself more assertively as one who governs his own existence. The appropriate pronoun to precede 'am' would be, not 'me', but 'I'. That more independent-sounding construction of '[I] am', though only half-achieved, does latently contradict the idea that Prometheus is passively being made to do whatever Jupiter chooses. Indeed, that shadowy 'I' almost allows 'hast thou made' to be read as Prometheus' claim that *he* has made *Jupiter*; that he himself has permitted, even compelled, this creature to become 'Monarch' (line 1); and to 'reign and triumph'.

Of course, the more obvious meaning of lines 10–11 is that Prometheus is the one being 'made' to 'reign' over a kingdom which is at first no more than the site of his own suffering. On this reading, Prometheus' 'triumph' here is no more than a cruel joke. As parody-king, whose reign consists of nothing but his 'own misery', the helpless Prometheus can seem more richly amusing to the 'scorn' of the truly triumphant Jupiter. But when Prometheus says 'to thy scorn', need he mean only something like 'for your arrogant amusement'? Could he instead mean something closer to 'in scorn of you' – 'to show you how confidently I spurn all your feeble attempts to make me feel defeated'? Perhaps Prometheus has come to 'reign' over his 'own misery' in a quite unironic sense. Perhaps he has learnt such self-control that Jupiter's attempts to make him suffer are reduced to an essentially '*vain*' revenge'.

I think this flickers only as a potential position, one which Prometheus cannot yet adopt. The verse paragraph does, after all, conclude with his confession that he is still being made to suffer:

> Ah me, alas, pain, pain ever, forever!
> No change, no pause, no hope! (lines 22–3)

Prometheus, here at least, sees no prospect of liberating himself. The possibility of an end to that regime which has seemed omnipotent for 'Three thousand years', is as invisible to the victim of that 'ill tyranny' as it is to the arrogant tyrant himself (lines 12, 19). Thus, 'eyeless in hate' (line 9) is aptly posed between 'me' and 'thou': equally able to refer back either to Prometheus or forward to Jupiter. Just as either could be the one who has 'made' the other in his own embittered image (line 10), so either may be the figure blinded by malice.

Before proceeding further with the poem, it will be useful to consider the first two paragraphs of Shelley's 'Preface' (Webb, pp. 29–30). Does their promise of a clear deviation from Aeschylus' model, and their promise of an ideal Prometheus, fit your own impression of the Prometheus whom we meet in the play's opening speech?

DISCUSSION

Whether we apply the more ambiguously positioned words in Prometheus' first speech to himself or to Jupiter, the vocabulary he deploys is surely drawn from the tyrant's own vicious, haughty rhetoric: 'foe', 'hate', 'reign', 'triumph', 'scorn', 'misery', 'revenge', 'pain', 'forever'. Such terminology might suggest that Prometheus is still at risk of coming to terms with Jupiter, of repeating what Shelley's Preface calls the 'feeble' resolution offered in Aeschylus' version. That ends by 'reconciling the Champion with the Oppressor of mankind'. Prometheus is there reduced to 'unsaying his high language, and quailing before his successful and perfidious enemy' (Webb, p. 30).

Shelley's own Prometheus, in this opening speech, may use a few terms from a liberatingly 'high language' – 'change' or 'hope'. These must be his own and cannot belong in Jupiter's low language of tyranny. However, each of these words is preceded by the 'no' which indeed constitutes an 'unsaying'.

The Preface perhaps also misleads in announcing a Prometheus who typifies 'the highest perfection of moral and intellectual nature, impelled by the purest and best motives to the best and noblest ends' (Webb, p. 30). This grandiloquent set of superlatives may apply only to what Prometheus could become; and to what he perhaps *has* become by the end of the play. At the beginning, our difficulty in telling him and Jupiter apart may be crucial. Consider, for instance, Prometheus' hypothesis: 'had I deigned to share ... thine ill tyranny'. Is that such a securely rejected scenario as it sounds? Or does Prometheus, later in the speech, still relapse into his own version of unhealthily tyrannical rhetoric? Consider these alternatives by re-reading lines 44–69.

DISCUSSION

Here, Prometheus does at first sound just as addicted as Jupiter is to the fantastical excitements of power. The 'crawling hours' are welcomed because eventually they will 'drag' down a rival. The opponent who is now able to play the 'cruel King' will be reduced to no more than a servile boot-licker. Conversely, Prometheus himself will then be so exalted that he will feel it beneath his dignity to 'trample ... such a prostrate slave'. Of course, Prometheus then claims to have blundered into a quite false account of his fantasies: 'Disdain? Ah no! I pity thee'. He asks to be interpreted as one speaking 'in grief/ Not exultation' or 'hate'. Finally, he announces his wish to 'recall' the bitter 'Curse' that he had once uttered against Jupiter.

This is clearly offered as a turning-point. But how large a change is involved? It is *after* the claim to 'pity' rather than 'Disdain', that Prometheus imagines the 'Ruin' that will hound his enemy down 'through wide Heaven'; and the 'terror' that will then cleave Jupiter's soul until it gapes 'like a Hell within'. Here, Prometheus himself deploys 'Heaven' and 'Hell': concepts which he has previously seen as Jupiter's: myths that encouraged 'barren hope' and 'fear', gulling pious 'slaves' into 'knee-worship, prayer and praise' of tyrants (lines 5–8). Perhaps, even at the very moment of resolving to feel 'pity' and to 'hate no more', Prometheus is still trapped in Jupiter's rhetoric of intimidation, is still bound to see the human world as ruled from above by a supreme 'Heaven' and threatened from below by the punishment-system of an eternal 'Hell'.

Alternatively, Prometheus *is* beginning to liberate himself; but can only do so by redefining words. He cannot empty his head of the vocabulary in which he thinks. He can only alter its implications. Some of the terms by which he is still bound gained their power in the past and now lurk only in his unconscious. Thus, he must 'recall' the terms of his 'Curse' first as an act of memory, summoning them back into his conscious mind. Only then will he be able to 'recall' them, in the other sense, retracting their bitterness, revoking their original meaning.

Other terms *have* remained part of his consciously deployed vocabulary and these he can already begin to revise. 'Heaven' and 'Hell' may exemplify such attempts at redefinition. 'Heaven', in line 54, has perhaps become a more neutrally topographical term. No longer associated with 'barren hope' of reward, it merely maps the vast cosmos which is the play's setting, evoking the 'wide' hunting-ground in which the historical process, after however many 'crawling hours', will inevitably bring 'ruin' even to the most seemingly stable situations. 'Hell', in line 56, has perhaps acquired a new, psychological meaning. Instead of being Christianity's literal place of punishment, this 'Hell within' may diagnose the 'terror' that can 'Gape' inside the mind's own self-torturing system of metaphor.

Some of the most potent metaphors which torment and humiliate us are those through which we see the external landscape: the supposedly 'real' world in which we so often feel we are bound to suffer. 'Mont Blanc', which is perhaps Shelley's most persuasive exposure of such ideas, seems to have supplied some of the landscape in which Prometheus describes his suffering. 'Solitude', so crucial in 'Mont Blanc' (lines 137–44), joins 'torture . . . Scorn and despair' to constitute a single 'empire' in *Prometheus Unbound* (lines 14–15); and the earlier poem's 'Earthquake-daemon' echoes amongst 'the Earthquake fiends' that reopen Prometheus' wounds (lines 38–9). Beneath the spreading glaciers of Mont Blanc, the 'dwelling-place/ Of insects, beasts' is 'forever gone' (lines 114–16). Prometheus describes his pain in terms of 'crawling glaciers' (line 31); while the 'mountain' to which he is chained seems so 'wintry, dead, unmeasured' that it too refuses any habitat to 'Insect, or beast'; and this is the observation that leads to his cry of 'pain . . . forever' (lines 20–4).

However, Shelley chooses not to situate the 'icy rocks' of *Prometheus Unbound*, in the European terrain of 'Mont Blanc'. Instead, they are placed at a far greater distance 'in the Indian Caucasus' (opening stage-direction); and line 64 stresses that Prometheus' curse echoed 'through India'. This shift to more mysterious territory discourages, at the outset, too literal a view of a landscape that is perhaps meant to be essentially psychological or symbolic. Moreover, the theory that human life itself had originated in central Asia was popular in Shelley's day. So the setting itself may imply that Prometheus is the archetype of all humanity.

The poem will later site the regeneration of human nature in the East. It also gives the heroine, whose actions initiate that regeneration, the name of Asia. It is 'her transforming presence' which has already turned another landscape as 'desolate and frozen' as the setting of Act I into 'sweet airs and sounds which flow/ Among the waters' (lines 828–31). Her power thus precisely echoes lines 120–6 of 'Mont Blanc' where the melting glaciers have power to dissolve and reshape the apparently unalterable landscape of traditional, European thought. Act I has Prometheus still trapped in Asia Minor, already poised to escape the bounds of familiar Europe but not yet able to fully enter the wholly different continent of attitudes where 'Asia waits in that far Indian vale' (line 826).

The setting neatly disassociates the poem from the idea that humanity in its highest forms is represented by white-skinned Europeans. That superstition underpinned the slave-trade and sanctioned the imperialist seizure of territories that had previously been inhabited only by other racial types. The Holy Alliance, conferring at their post-Waterloo summits, not only decided to postpone the abolition of the slave-trade but also shared out various foreign territories that could be usefully exploited. At these 'Kingly conclaves', human 'blood' was indeed 'bought and sold' for 'gold' (lines 530–1). The most controversially profitable of Britain's recent expansions had been in India itself; and there it had, of course, been native Indians, rather than any of the invading Europeans, who had ended up languishing in chains.

However, the native cultures that were being treated so scorn-

fully by those who meant to subjugate the Indian sub-continent were
already being described admiringly by some British authors.[5]
Perhaps, the setting implies that Europeans can actively learn from
Asian societies; that Western habits of thought are in some respects
inferior to the attitudes embodied in Eastern religion and culture.

Christianity, which was so central to the culture of Shelley's
Europe, pervades the rhetoric of Act I. You might make yourself a list
of quotations which explicitly refer to Jesus or deploy terms (such as
'The saviour' in line 817) which have specifically Christian associations in other contexts, however different their usage here. Lines
546–65 might be a centre-piece; but you should be able to find
many other, briefer examples; and their ambiguities are worth
noting. For instance, that 'youth/ With patient looks nailed to a
crucifix' (line 585) could be Jesus; or the still unliberated Prometheus; or merely one, anonymous example drawn from those count-
less victims of Church propaganda, the 'self-despising slaves of
Heaven' whom Prometheus, if he is to be a true 'saviour . . . of
suffering man' must rescue (lines 429, 817).

But Prometheus, of course, only represents what is our own
potential. Each reader is invited to accept that it is his or her own
'destiny to be,/ The saviour and the strength of suffering man' (lines
816–17). How far we can act upon that responsibility will depend,
Shelley implies, upon our ability to learn some new, at first foreign-
sounding, language: one utterly alien to the discourse now current in
Europe where prattle about 'Heaven' makes us 'self-despising slaves'
on earth.

The Judaeo-Christian tradition of European culture has tended
to put great emphasis upon speech, to centre its self-confidence on an
ability to describe experience in verbal language: 'In the beginning
was the Word'. This logocentricity cannot be escaped by *Prometheus
Unbound* which is obviously addressing itself, through words, to a
European audience. But the poem does pose the disturbing hypothesis that we sometimes use words to talk ourselves out of, rather than
into, any accurate understanding.

For instance, before the poem opens, Prometheus has already
cursed Jupiter: in words. Did those words merely describe some
pre-existing enemy to human happiness? Or did those words actively
create the mere fantasy of such a foe? Prometheus says: 'The curse/ I
breathed on thee I would recall'; and, according to the West's
creation-myth in Genesis, it was indeed an act of breathing which
gave life. To the extent that 'recall' means, not revoke, but remember, could Prometheus mean to relish once more those words of
creative hatred? Does he want to relive that moment of god-like
power in which his curse constructed such a convincing image
of loathsome tyranny that it indeed 'breathed' life into a new
species?

Consider some other lines that focus on the power of speech itself:

> If then my words had power
> – Though I am changed so that aught evil wish
> Is dead within, although no memory be
> Of what is hate – let them not lose it now!
> What was that curse? for ye all heard me speak.   (lines 69–73)

> I hear a sound of voices – not the voice
> Which I gave forth.   (lines 113–14)

> Why answer ye not, still?   (line 129)

> . . . for I would hear that curse again   (line 131)

> . . . mine own words, I pray, deny me not   (line 190)

>   . . . let not aught
> Of that which may be evil, pass again
> My lips, or those of aught resembling me. –
> Phantasm of Jupiter, arise, appear,   (lines 218–21)

To some extent, this last line does perhaps echo a sinister creativity in Prometheus' original curse.

However, the need to conjure up a phantom Jupiter to voice such rage may derive from the fact that Prometheus is now in an almost opposite frame of mind. For Prometheus himself to remember and describe again may be impossible because it would be to *re*present what is now lost in a safely irrecoverable past. That earlier vindictiveness may be so alien to his new way of thinking that he cannot himself any longer speak the language which gives such malice definition.

Perhaps Prometheus is already sufficiently advanced in love to have forgotten the grammar of competitiveness which passes for common sense amongst more ordinary mortals. Earth tells him:

>   thou canst not hear:
> Thou art immortal, and this tongue is known
> Only to those who die . . .   (lines 149–51)

She asks:

>   How canst thou hear
> Who knowest not the language of the dead?   (lines 138–9)

Earth herself did hear the curse; and, unlike Prometheus, her 'seas and streams,/ Mountains and caves and winds' still remember it. They, with 'the inarticulate people of the dead/ Preserve' it as 'a treasured spell'; and:

>   meditate
> In secret joy and hope those dreadful words
> But dare not speak them.   (lines 179–86)

How literally are words like 'immortal' or 'dead' being used here? Clearly, a tyrant-defying spirit in humanity can outlast any particular individual or generation. Conversely, energy as destructive as Jupiter's may make those who are still physically alive feel so dispirited that they are virtually dead.

Earth, however lasting the ecosystem as a whole may be, is composed of perishable parts. So, she may here speak for a more resignedly mortal point of view than Prometheus himself needs to adopt. As Prometheus grows into symbolizing all that is of lasting worth in his species, he perhaps becomes less corruptible by the forces of death than Earth for whom 'dreadful words' of hate are still a 'secret joy' to be hoarded. Prometheus does, at least partly, mean to 'recall' his curse so as to revoke it. Earth's reaction to this gesture of life-giving humanitarianism is perversely one of grief, as if she is bereaved. Prometheus' mercy is misinterpreted as servility; and his moral victory is treated by Earth simply as military defeat:

> Misery, O misery to me
> That Jove should vanquish thee

> * * *

> Howl, Spirits of the living and the dead,
> Your refuge, your defence lies fallen and vanquished.

> (lines 306–11)

Her bitter cry is followed by First and Second Echo repeating 'fallen and vanquished'. It is only Ione, equipped with memory of earlier apparent setbacks, who can see Prometheus' present imprisonment as no more than 'some passing spasm' (line 314).

How should we relate 'the dead' of lines 139 and 183 (whose language cannot be shared by the now essentially living Prometheus) with the composite phrase 'the living and the dead' in line 305? Perhaps, in this last expression, Earth merely refers to that complex blend of survival and extinction which comprises her own natural world. But she could here be pointing to that other, far more subterranean 'world . . . of life and death': the one which contains 'shadows of all forms' that function in the normal, visible world of so-called reality. There are varying interpretations of this key-passage about the 'two worlds of life and death' (lines 195–209). It may image the relationship between Prometheus' conscious thoughts (about both himself and others) and that subliminal theatre, deep in his unconscious. There another, more surreal, image of his own body hangs as 'a writhing shade' (line 203); and another image of his enemy, sits on a 'throne/ Of burning gold'. The unconscious supposedly equivocates in its attitude to father-figures; and here both dazzled admiration and sadistic longings to depose could be evoked by 'the supreme tyrant's' throne so ambiguously 'burning' (lines 208–9).

However, it may be that here too the words of the poem are interested in their own power. This second world of images need not be in any sense a secondary one. It could be the crucial arena of language in which all our actions are conceived or abandoned.

Certainly, Prometheus is dissatisfied with an image which he has so far merely made visible, and not yet invested with the power of words. So long as the Phantasm can only be seen and not heard, its Ozymandias-like image of tyranny seems frustratingly inadequate:

> I see the curse on gestures proud and cold,
> And looks of firm defiance, and calm hate,
> And such despair as mocks itself with smiles,
> Written as on a scroll . . . yet speak – O speak!   (lines 258–61)

However, the poem is so ambivalent as to whether words are more likely to reveal or to conceal mankind's higher destiny, that no sooner has the Phantom spoken than Prometheus decides:

> It doth repent me: words are quick and vain;
> Grief for awhile is blind, and so was mine.
> I wish no living thing to suffer pain.   (lines 303–5)

Here at last, Prometheus does perhaps achieve a genuine alteration in his attitudes.

Rejecting one set of words which can articulate nothing but blindness, he finds, in the very different words of line 305 an insight into his own deepest wishes. The simple assertion bespeaks at once both a sturdy self-confidence and an all-embracing tenderness for others. It arguably begins the process of dismantling those fantasies from which absolute power derives; and on which a figure like Jupiter depends for his very existence.

You may think that I have exaggerated the extent to which the Phantasm of Jupiter can be read as a product of Prometheus' own words; and have conversely underplayed its evocation of a real power in contemporary politics. Certainly, the Phantasm is discovered 'on his throne' (line 208); and is soon equipped with both a 'sceptre' (line 235) and a 'crown' (line 290). Moreover, his agents, the Furies, are to be 'ministers of pain and fear' in ways that could seem highly topical. Shelley's first readers, thanks to the policies of the British government's ministers had, for many years, lived on an island surrounded by the 'red gulphs of war' (line 257). Their newspapers had constantly reported how 'Shipwreck' made the sea as much of a killing-ground as the land where 'cities sink howling in ruin' (line 499).

The more optimistic Spirits cannot ignore these horrors of naval warfare. They can only claim that isolated gestures of human decency can still occur:

Mighty fleets were strewn like chaff
And spread beneath, a hell of death
O'er the white waters. I alit
On a great ship lightning-split
And speeded hither on the sigh
Of one who gave an enemy
His plank – then plunged aside to die.   (lines 716–22)

This generous compassion for an enemy clearly echoes Prometheus' own resolve that 'no living thing' should 'suffer pain'. But the sailor's gesture is made at the cost of his own life. War-mongering leaders, on both sides, once the French Revolution had declined into Napoleonic dictatorship, were not likely to even hear about, let alone be converted by, such a localized act. And yet they had clearly not been mere figments of some embittered individual's imagination. They had been too indisputably destructive of human lives for a Phantasm ordering 'a hell of death' to be understood as fantasy. It clearly represents forces as factual as those that had confined prisoners in the Bastille until they were rescued by the revolutionaries. Nevertheless, a major alteration in the way that subjects do imagine the king's power relative to their own, had inevitably been a prerequisite of that revolution.

Some passages of Act I refer far more explicitly to the French Revolution and yet, even here, verbal language may be a key-issue again. Please now read again lines 564–77, (Webb, p. 49); lines 646–54 (Webb, p. 51); and lines 694–707 (Webb, pp. 52–3).

DISCUSSION

Speech surely does matter in these passages too: even if it is only one of the two great 'woes:/ To speak, and to behold' (lines 646–7). The words of the revolutionaries' mantra seem inadequate. 'Truth, Liberty, and Love' (line 651) turn out to presage 'strife, deceit and fear' (line 576). In the 'mingled din' initiated by the 'battle-trumpet', the shout of 'Freedom!' may be synonymous with 'Hope!'; but both sides are presumably howling 'Death!' to each other; and we cannot tell which ends up able to chant 'Victory!' of (lines 694, 700–1). All such militant slogans can slide into the merely militaristic; and may ultimately serve the interests of the counter-revolution. They have, significantly, 'faded' into silence before a more secure, less verbal, 'sound' can express the true 'soul of love' (lines 702–4). It is, after all, a wordless 'sigh' which articulates the exemplary compassion of the sailor saving his enemy in line 720.

Such distinctions may prepare the way for a movement towards Act II where Asia will offer her 'music . . . / Of . . . *wordless* converse . . . the *sense* with which love talks' (Act II, Scene i, lines 52–3).

Already, in Act I, Prometheus implies that his lack of this supra-
verbal love is virtually synonymous with the absence of Asia:

> How fair these air-born shapes! And yet I feel
> Most vain all hope but love, and thou art far,
> Asia.   (Act I, lines 807–9)

Nevertheless, the very medium of literature in which Prometheus
exists requires his visionary love, as well as his blind hate, to be
expressed in words. The poem suggests that we cannot turn our
backs on unreliable speech and hope to understand some wholly
separate, 'real' world. Even its most literal events – revolution and
war – may be caused or prevented by attitudes which do depend on
words: on the terms in which people describe themselves; or their
situation; or their own power to alter it.

Act I may allow Prometheus to save his own mind from the corruption of responding to hatred only with hatred. Nevertheless, his body
remains bound and he cannot yet act to save others. For that, almost
indescribably vaster, transformation, the poem turns in the second
Act from the male Prometheus whose terminology often reflects
traditional, European assumptions to the female Asia. The first scene
of Act II displays the feminine, wholly uncompetitive affection that
Asia and her two sisters feel for each other and for the absent
Prometheus. Their co-operation, sharing erotic dreams as well as
political aspirations, leads Asia and Panthea to set out on a quest. In
the second scene, they are drawn on by a chorus 'Of echoes'. These
evoke 'Demogorgon's mighty law' of historical necessity: a dream-
like sound which 'Attracts' and 'impels' people, even when they are
under the illusion that it is their own 'desires' which determine their
actions (lines 42–57). Yet literature itself, recalling past glories and
prophesying those yet to come, may form one crucial set of cogs in
this great machine for manufacturing the future: it is 'wise and lovely
songs' that summon the travellers on towards the knowledge that
'the chained Titan . . . shall be loosed and make the Earth/ One
brotherhood' (lines 91–7).

The next scene is set on 'A Pinnacle of Rock among Mountains'
where a 'mighty portal/ Like a volcano's meteor-breathing chasm'
leads 'to the realm of Demogorgon'. From this:

> the oracular vapour is hurled up
> Which lonely men drink wandering in their youth,
> And call truth, virtue, love, genius or joy,
> That maddening wine of life.   (Act II, Scene iii, lines 1–7)

The oracle may, at present, provoke aspirations that seem to isolate
and derange.

However, its setting presages a cumulative joining of forces. The snowscape here, like that of 'Mont Blanc' may at first seem daunting: 'continuous, vast,/ Awful as silence'. Yet Asia can hear the seismic rumblings of massive change:

> Hark! the rushing snow!
> The sun-awakened avalanche! whose mass,
> Thrice lifted by the storm, had gathered there
> Flake after flake, in heaven-defying minds
> As thought by thought is piled, till some great truth
> Is loosened, and the nations echo round,
> Shaken to their roots, as do the mountains now.
>
> (Act II, Scene iii, lines 35–42)

This pregnant landscape which is so indissolubly both mental and literal prepares the way for the next scene where Asia and Panthea enter the very 'cave of Demogorgon' to consult him as an oracle.

Here, at last, Asia imagines and awakes what has hitherto been 'a world unknown' where 'sleeps a voice unspoken' (Act II scene i, lines 190–1). Yet, when Demogorgon's voice is finally aroused, its answers are enigmatically terse: perhaps to challenge the premises of Asia's questions.

Asia does represent an ideal in the work as a whole; but she may here have to speak on behalf of those whose thoughts are still trapped in current speech-patterns. Though she herself may already know better, the questions through which she approaches Demogorgon may have to echo the kinds of question that the reader might ask. You may anyway decide that Demogorgon's replies, though brief and apparently evasive, do prove highly revealing.

Please now read Act II scene iv (Webb, pp. 57–61).

DISCUSSION

Demogorgon's own gloss – 'I spoke but as ye speak' (line 112) – invites us to hear his voice as that of an echo-chamber. If so, does it reinforce some special insights that Asia can already articulate? Or does it amplify no more than those more traditional patterns of speech and thought which she still shares with the rest of us? The 'ye' has associations of the plural. So, the present tense of 'speak' could be the continuing present in which Shelley's first readers tend to go on asking the old questions, using a rhetoric of approach which may actively prevent their reaching more liberating answers.

Those comfortably pious enquiries about the creation of the world (line 9), or of human love (lines 12–18) may allow no more fruitful answer than Demogorgon's curt nods to 'God' and to those traditional responses which describe him as both 'Almighty' and 'Merciful' (lines 9, 11, 18). Conversely, to question the origins of 'self-contempt' (line 25) may be to allow for a more thought-provokingly open-ended conclusion: 'He reigns' (line 28). The possibility that 'He' here could mean Prometheus, as well as Jupiter, has been anticipated, not only by much in Act I, but also by Asia's own equivocal phrasing in her question. She already implies, in asking about 'terror' (line 19), that it could derive either from a genuine external threat or merely from internal habits of feeling: 'Hell, or the sharp fear of Hell' (line 28). She already suggests, when claiming to be baffled about the origin of 'Pain' that human suffering, being '*unheeded* and *familiar speech*', derives partly from our caring so little about each other; and partly from that habitual rhetoric through which we literally talk ourselves into 'Pain' (line 26).

To achieve a dialogue – and so make dialectical progress towards new truth – Asia may scarcely need the responses of an external voice like Demogorgon's. She may herself contain two voices. With one, she is still human enough to ask a silly question. With the other, she already anticipates our hitherto suppressed, true humanity; and can thus pose a subtler question that implicitly exposes the inadequacy of the first.

From Demogorgon, she gets in reply to her first question ('Who made the living world?') no more than the bleakly monosyllabic reply of 'God' (line 9). His contribution here may merely be to frustrate her into finding a better answer: that the 'world' that is relevantly 'living' was not created by God; but, on the contrary, is still being created by men and women. Her second question about the world shows that she has been provoked into glossing 'all/ That it contains', not as material objects, but as the intellectual and emotional energy of human beings: 'thought, passion, reason, will,/ Imagination' (lines 9–11).

The dialogue may be driving Asia towards such an appreciation of human power that she might one day challenge Jupiter himself with that bold question which closes 'Mont Blanc':

> And what wert thou, and earth, and stars, and sea,
> If to the human mind's imaginings
> Silence and solitude were vacancy?

Meanwhile, Asia may have little cause to feel satisfied with the human imagination so long as it still abuses itself by filling vacancy with bogeymen like Jupiter.

Even when she has talked herself forward into the recognition that the source of evil is 'Not Jove' (lines 100–6), she still believes in him; and she still seeks to understand Jupiter's existence in terms of his own dotty rhetoric, trying to tell things apart by discriminating between the hierarchical alternatives of ruler and ruled: 'Declare/ Who is his master? Is he too a slave?' (lines 108–9). Demogorgon replies: 'All spirits are enslaved who serve things evil'; and then immediately tells his human questioner that she is, almost by definition, the expert on such spirits: 'Thou knowest if Jupiter be such or no' (lines 110–11).

Demogorgon's example of what it is like for him to speak as she herself speaks is the servile slogan, 'Jove is the supreme of living things' (lines 113–14). To the extent that this is the language still used by those who seek Demogorgon's knowledge, he may be compelled to frustrate them by insisting that 'the deep truth is imageless' – at least in the verbal imagery available to contemporary rhetoric. For the present, 'a voice/ Is wanting' (lines 115–16).

However, Demogorgon arguably does have ways of at least hinting some answers. He may signal a definition of that still awaited 'voice', in the etymology of his name which suggests 'People-Monster'. There was also a radical journal circulating in England at the time called *The Gorgon*; and its readers were mainly working-class. The implication may be that adequate reform cannot successfully be announced by an elite of upper-class intellectuals: those who might feel most able to make sense of the other voices in this sophisticated reworking of a Greek drama. Instead, revolution must arise from the ordinary, working people of England, whose voice, once found, may sound to refined ears as baffling, or as monstrous, as Demogorgon's does here.

Moreover, even when sounding least helpful, he manages to educate Asia; or, more precisely, to teach her how to teach herself. Consider, for instance, that two-word answer, 'He reigns' (line 31). The informative pronoun (patriarchy is enthroned in all contemporary institutions) is followed by an even more suggestive verb: for the time being, that verb's present tense implies, power *is* in the hands of monarchy and of its various allies in Church and State. Demogorgon's refusal to identify the 'He' more specifically – to 'Utter his name' (line 29) – does provoke Asia into livelier curiosity about what the actual exercise of such power means. Anyone who 'reigns' prevents others acquiring 'knowledge' and fulfilling their intellectual potential. He deprives them of that confidence which would come from controlling their own destiny and exercising their full capacity for affection. He who reigns over an empire, as His Majesty, denies his subjects what is their own inborn nature, refuses them 'The birthrights of their being . . . *Self*-empire, and the majesty of *love*' (lines 38–42).

Demogorgon's refusal of a name saves Asia from concentrating too narrowly on any one of those, many brand-names under which power operates – that 'succession of tyrants . . . from Robespierre to Louis XVIII' in which 'demagogues . . . and legitimate kings are merely varieties of the same class'.[6] She is forced towards a larger definition of the type who 'reigns': one that can include, for instance, both Napoleon and his supposed opponent, George IV. Both war-mongers could embody those 'mad disquietudes . . . which levied

mutual war' (lines 65–75). The fate of either could epitomise what
Asia discovers is the meaning of power:

> To know nor faith nor love nor law, to be
> Omnipotent but friendless, is to reign;   (lines 47–8)

Demogorgon's reluctance to name names may even signal his fear
that Asia herself could be tempted towards the vengefulness that
corrupted the French Revolution. Certainly, one critic suspects Asia
of wanting the name so that she can use it as a lethal spell in cursing
the culprit. On this reading, Demogorgon is simply saving her from
the very error which we have already seen chaining the tortured
Prometheus down as a mirror-image of his vindictive oppressor.[7]

That view would make Asia Demogorgon's pupil. However, it
has also been argued that their roles are quite the reverse; that
Demogorgon, imaging the still inert proletariat, is himself gradually
being roused and educated by Asia, acting as a radical orator:

> Prometheus, she reminds him, has given humanity many wonderful
> gifts: science; the power to beat the elements; love; speech; music; the
> ability to build cities; the possibility of cooperation between people of
> different races ('and the Celt knew the Indian' [line 94]). For all this,
> Prometheus 'hangs withering in destined pain'. Her magnificent
> speech ends where it started by demanding to know 'who rains down
> evil'. She refuses to accept another answer of 'God' or 'Jupiter'. . . She
> knows that there *is* something more powerful than tyranny: a united
> and risen people. Her problem is to breathe a spirit of confidence and
> unity into the shapeless Demogorgon . . .[8]

Need these two views as to which is the pupil be mutually exclusive?
Perhaps both the intellectual orator (whether she begins with demands for a named culprit to punish; or with rather glib, rhetorical
questions) *and* the initially surly working-class could learn from each
other.

Demogorgon may anyway image a larger force. This could
include a growth in political awareness amongst the labouring class,
but only as one of many factors constituting a pressure towards
change. He may represent the passage of time itself: as that would be
understood in the 'doctrine of Necessity' which Shelley had extracted
from Godwin. According to this, 'there is neither good nor evil in the
universe, otherwise than as we apply the epithets'. So writes Shelley
in a note glossing lines in *Queen Mab* where 'Necessity' is told: 'thou/
Regardest . . . all with an impartial eye . . . / Because thou hast not
human sense . . . thou art not human mind'.[9] History may develop
along its inexorable path according to laws no more humane than the
laws of physics. If so, Demogorgon is understandably reluctant to
talk of God or morality. Doing so misrepresents his own essentially
impartial nature: which is that of natural laws; not of man-made
theology, or of language-defined human feeling.

Revolution, Shelley sometimes hoped, would eventually emerge by a process as inevitable as Darwinian evolution:

> a new race has arisen throughout Europe, nursed in the abhorrence of the opinions which are its chains, and she will continue to produce fresh generations to accomplish that destiny which tyrants foresee and dread.[10]

Demogorgon can be seen as Jupiter's child:[11] the inevitably different generation of the future. Yet the change that he initiates is neither the mere inheriting of his father's throne; nor even an act of usurpation in which he prematurely installs himself in that power-base. Instead, he obliterates it, permanently.

The revolutionary moment, as the 'shadow of a destiny/ More dread' is like the soaring smoke of the mightiest volcanic explosion: its 'darkness' will 'ascend' so high as to 'wrap in lasting night Heaven's *kingless* throne' (lines 139–49). If a 'throne' came to mean one on which no ruler would ever again sit, the word would lose all its current meaning and power; just as a 'Heaven' in which no God could any longer be seen would have been emptied of its present significance. Demogorgon soon becomes almost indistinguishable from this revolutionary moment. Just like the Spirit of that explosive Hour, he too is a 'terrible shadow' who 'floats/ Up'. As 'the lurid smoke/ Of earth-quake-ruined cities', the monster too 'ascends . . . Blackening the night' (lines 150–5).

This eruption of wild energy, uniting the monster with its moment, bursts into the poem so suddenly that it almost seems a direct result of the questions asked by Panthea. Her reaction to it is 'Thus I am answered' (line 155). Perhaps the implication is that, if literature can once phrase the truly challenging question, querying the very bases of traditional power in sufficiently cogent terms, then the demand will instantly be answered. Radical poetry about the future would, at its most potent, be a precisely self-fulfilling prophecy. Indeed, one critic interprets Demogorgon as no more than 'a projection of this capacity to imagine with hope, and by naming, to make that hope a reality'.[12]

Certainly, Shelley was attracted by Godwin's deterministic view that intellectual progress amongst an elite would automatically lead one day to a just society. But Shelley also saw the risk of putting so much faith in the ultimate power of radical thought and literature that any immediate political activism could be avoided as superfluous. The theory provided such a convenient rationale for doing nothing, even when some of the chains which bound one's contemporaries were all too literal. So, if Demogorgon's ascent does represent the violent eruption of a working-class who are no longer willing to be fobbed off with promises, it might derive from Shelley's momentarily nerving himself in 1819 to accept that action, however violent, was the only adequate answer to the needs evoked by Asia's questions.

However, you need to consider the two kinds of chariot which are introduced at line 130 and then distinguished as one in which that 'ghastly charioteer', the Spirit 'of dreadful countenance', is joined by Demogorgon (lines 142–53); and another which 'waits for Panthea' (line 141). This second chariot, or 'car', is described in lines 156–62. Might these two vehicles represent precisely the alternatives of a revolution so hideously violent that it must be forestalled; and a series of gradual reforms, sanctified by Asia's love? The task Shelley would then be setting his audience would be to ensure that Asia's chariot of peaceful regeneration could be made to move fast enough so that the proletariat would be willing to await its arrival. The next scene of the poem does show Asia's apparent inability to accelerate the chariot in which she travels (Act II, scene v, lines 3–7).

That scene, like the vast majority of the poem's ensuing scenes, is not included in Webb's selection which finds space only for one, short extract from each of the last two Acts. Ideally, of course, you should obtain a text of the entire work. However, this is not a story of causally linked events recalled from the past; but a loosely structured hymn of prophecy about future ways of thinking, of feeling, and (perhaps most crucially) of speaking and writing. So, fragments, even when unsupported by their original context, can be hugely moving.

Moreover, each of Webb's two final extracts was composed to stand as the poem's last lines. The Spirit of the Hour's speech which closes Act III had originally been planned as the last part of a three-act poem which was duely completed in April, 1819. Shelley did not decide to add a fourth Act until September. When he completed it in December, the entire text of the expanded poem now ended with Demogorgon's speech.

In each of these extracts then, Shelley may be attempting to recapitulate the central concerns of the poem. But you should explore style as well as substance here, particularly in the second passage. The technical brilliance of the poem, its subtle and yet forceful manipulation of sound and syntax, is perhaps nowhere more worth exploring. Please read both extracts now: Webb, pages 63–4, lines 54–94; lines 1–25.

DISCUSSION

The textual history in which, at different stages, both the Spirit of the Hour and Demogorgon have the last word seems apt enough: the passing hours that constitute the historical process itself are clearly one of the forces which Demogorgon, that flexibly amorphous monster, represents. He may also image the common people as they at last achieve enough political consciousness to discover their united power, articulating demands for democracy in a voice that can no longer be ignored. But on this reading too, a particular, future moment (or the 'Spirit' that informs and creates it) could be almost interchangeably identified with the working-class whose self-definition and power it initiates.

The Spirit of the Hour's speech surely does recapitulate, in more confidently triumphant tones, the insights and aspirations that were so central even to the most apparently static moments of earlier scenes. Tyrannical power may now be a scarcely remembered night-mare, rather than an inescapably present reality. But, the poetry still strives to disassociate power from particular persons. Here too, society is not ruled by some named individual whose impact might reflect his own, singularly impressive strength. Instead, social control is elusively distributed amongst myriad institutions: political, religious and legal.

The significantly plural nouns of 'Thrones, altars, judgement-seats, and prisons' have no qualifying adjectives to distinguish their roles; or to lend any false colour to what has been an unqualified conspiracy of equally shabby forces. They are hurled down in a dismissive list. The arbitrary-sounding order in which they are thrown together recalls the promiscuous relationships that formed their covert alliance: the pretty, theatrical props of 'Sceptres, tiaras' were inseparable from the ugly palpabilities of 'swords, and chains'. And these in turn derived their power from words: whole 'tomes/ Of reasoned wrong' that indoctrinated ordinary people into an illusion that they were helpless (lines 54–7).

That ubiquitous rhetoric, through which oppression operated, disguising its 'savage' workings 'under many a name' (lines 71–2) now seems as anachronistic as Ozymandias' inscription. Sym-bols that once claimed to epitomize the most refined heights of civilization are now scorned as essentially primitive: 'monstrous and barbaric shapes, / The ghosts of a no-more-remembered fame' (lines 58–9). All these, the Spirit asserts bluntly, 'Were Jupiter' (line 73).

However, earlier scenes have led us to expect that 'Jupiter' will mask, not only the callousness of earthly rulers, but also the gutless-ness of their subjects. So, the lines that here immediately follow the naming of Jupiter do not recall some singularly potent ruler. Instead they remember those plural victims whose servility was the real 'tyrant of the world' (line 73): whole 'nations, panic-stricken', myriad 'hearts . . . Flattering the thing they feared, which fear was hate' (lines 75–8). Their own rhetoric 'imaged to the pride of kings and priests' that 'dark yet mighty faith' in hierarchy. Their vocabulary compulsively discriminated people into either ruler or ruled: creating that mutual misery in which those who wear 'tiaras' and those who wear 'chains' are equally 'wretched men' (lines 55–6).

Yet, in spite of the poem's prophetic imaginings, that woefully limited language is still the language of the anticipated reader. Its terms must thus be deployed and yet denied. Shelley achieves this in his brilliant use of negatives: 'Sceptreless . . . uncircumscribed . . . unclassed . . . tribeless . . . nationless' (lines 84–5).

It is the sheer versatility of technique that makes these lines so rousing. The device of subverting a word within itself by adding a negative suffix ('-less') or prefix ('un'-) is followed by a trio of corrupting terms, 'awe, worship, degree' still in their unadapted forms; but preceded by the 'Exempt from' which deprives them of power before they appear. Before that can settle into a pattern, we return to the use of a negative suffix, but now one deployed for opposite purposes: to raise the possibility of a cancellation; and then to dismiss it – 'Passionless? no . . .'. Then this same line invigoratingly returns to the 'Exempt from . . .', formula in a version sufficiently variant to seem fresh: ' . . . – yet free from guilt or pain' (line 87).

These two experiences are 'made or suffered' by the 'will' of 'man' who is now securely the subject of the speech. The passage began with institutions, inanimate objects and oppressive symbols. These governed all the verbs up to line 73. By the end, brotherhood has united the dividedly plural 'wretched men' (line 55) into singular 'man': introduced in line 84, and insisted upon again in line 87. Shelley's craftsmanship allows us to hear, in the very grammar of the poem, that government has passed from 'Sceptres, tiaras, swords' to man himself. He, or 'his will', governs all four verbs in these last lines. It is he who, now that the 'mask' of Jupiter, with all its 'Thrones, altars, judgement-seats, and prisons' has vanished, 'remains' (line 84). It is he, not some external God, who has created and permitted: 'made, or suffered' (line 89). And, perhaps most crucially, it is he who has found a way of turning his own, once degrading, language inside out: so that now the discourse of regality allows him to feel 'the king/ Over himself' (line 87). So too the rhetoric of servitude is now recycled to convey only his own power over 'chance and death' – 'ruling them like slaves' (lines 90–1).

Yet, from these, he is explicitly not yet exempt. Man is still chained down to earth by these 'clogs' of mortality and 'mutability'; even if, without them, he 'might oversoar/ The loftiest star of unascended Heaven' (lines 91–3). The poem's last verb is thus forlornly conditional. The humanity which is its subject governs an over-reaching action of which it can only dream. Here, in 'unascended', the negative prefix cancels what would be a lovely aspiration. This clearly contrasts with those earlier negative epithets, like 'uncircumscribed' or 'unclassed', so cheering in their elimination of the ugly divisions that once bound humanity down. The final lines, in using the passage's syntactical and lexical devices to such different effect, confirm the poem's own triumphant versatility; even as they soberly acknowledge that no revolution will free human beings from change and death. Whatever we could achieve as a community, we still seem bound to care about others, and about ourselves, as individuals.

So, 'guilt or pain' will go on being 'suffered'. If we read 'suffered' retrospectively in the light of the last lines, it may mean, not 'permitted', but 'miserably endured'. The ambivalence announced early in Act I is in fact alive to the very end. Here too, suffering may be neither a fantasy nor the merely transient product of a political regime. Beneath the sky-assaulting confidence of this closing hymn to mankind, we can still hear Prometheus' original fear that pain may mean nothing less than itself; and that it could prove a lasting feature of human experience: 'pain, pain ever, forever' (Act I, line 23).

Demogorgon's speech, which closes the final version of the play, also faces the possibility that Jupiter's overthrow, which he celebrates in the first stanza, may not guarantee a lasting elimination of unhappiness. 'Eternity', for Demogorgon, is not some sterile stasis but the limitlessly fertile energy of the historical process: the 'Mother of many acts and hours' (lines 11–12). As such, it may permit even the birth of future Jupiters who might grow into emperors as monstrous. So, Demogorgon, braced for such future disasters, devotes two-thirds of his speech (lines 9–25) to practising the 'spells' with which 'to re-assume/ An empire o'er the disentangled doom' (lines 15–16).

Here again, in designing such a transforming context for a term like 'empire', Shelley finds ways of using the current language of corruptly hierarchical society to energise those who should dismantle it. In the last line, following 'Life, Joy' and all that has gone before, 'Empire' appears again with 'Victory'. Both words now mean almost the opposite of what they had meant to the imperialist victors of Waterloo. Similarly, the 'awful throne' is, in Demogorgon's vision, now occupied by 'Love' and before we can hear about 'power', it has been given the redefinition of that preceding adjective, 'patient' (line 4).

Nouns and adjectives, which are in themselves quite simple, gain extraordinary resonance in this passage from the sentence-structures in which they are deployed and, above all, from the verbs that they govern. A noun like 'Conquest' is caught in the very act of self-destruction as it 'is dragged captive' (line 3). We can hear how 'patient' is 'Love', in accumulating its 'power', as we read through the six phrases that follow its introduction at the beginning of line 4. The tension coiled into the syntax by these is not released by the main verb until the end of line 7. There, at last, we discover what Love does; and the sentence's gathered energy suddenly erupts in the carefully chosen verb, 'Springs'. In other contexts, this verb's evocation of instantly launched strength might evoke the predatory leap of a tiger; but it is here immediately followed by another verb that gives it an extra, punning power: 'springs/ And folds over the world its healing wings'. Love, as a bird tenderly enfolding a brood that is the entire planet, reminds us that spring means also a time of year: the breeding season that ends a sterile winter. Love thus also 'springs' as that massive shift in light and temperature which transforms the earth and all life upon it.

A similar accretion of power can be seen in the second stanza whose opening line consists of nothing but four unqualified nouns. Their strength can then be heard growing through the whole of an 8-line sentence: an incantation that chants out their significance until we do hear those, originally unadorned, nouns as potent 'spells' (line 25).

In the final stanza, massed verbs, in the infinitive case, voice the stamina of that energy which will neither 'change, nor falter, nor repent' but continue 'To suffer . . . To forgive . . . To defy . . . To Love, and bear' (lines 16–20). Before this perpetual motion runs any risk of seeming monotonous, the grammar modulates, from another infinitive, into a more decisive assertion:

> to hope, till Hope creates
> From its own wreck the thing it contemplates;   (lines 20–1)

The rhyme here insists on the partnership of creative action and the more contemplative side of a politically committed intellectual's existence. The power of Hope to make a new 'thing', to transform that material world of human society where our fellow human beings suffer so needlessly is given priority in 'creates'. But, when that word's matching chime is supplied by 'contemplates', our ability to act effectively sounds inseparable from our more meditative role as readers. We can only make new things happen by weaning ourselves away from old ways of seeing and speaking: habits which validate a resigned inertia. A new society can only be built by those who have learnt to think their way out of the despair created by the 'wreck' of earlier optimisms.

For Shelley's first readers, the apparent wreck of a capitalised 'Hope' must evoke nothing less than the recent political and intellectual history of Europe: the apparently irreparable demolition of that idealistic optimism that had brought revolution to France. The poem, in its Preface, promises 'a passion for reforming the world'; but it there also implicitly acknowledges that its upper-class audience now tends to contemplate such hopes with a jaundiced eye. Action depends on those 'select classes of poetical readers' having their minds, in the fullest sense, changed.

Shelley's explicit 'purpose', according to the Preface is 'to familiarise the highly refined imagination' of an elite with 'beautiful idealisms'. These have come to seem such self-evident rubbish that they are now scarcely noticed by the cultured mind that scorns them. Yet Shelley knows only too well:

> that until the mind can love, and admire, and trust, and hope, and endure, reasoned principles of moral conduct are seeds cast upon the highway of life which the unconscious passenger tramples into dust, although they would bear the harvest of his happiness.
>
> (Webb, pp. 32–3)

This passage not only takes us back to where we began in that 'gloom and misanthropy' which dominated European, post-revolutionary minds in Shelley's maturity. It also recalls many of the other poems that we have considered. For instance, its image of radical literature as prophetic seeds to be harvested by some future generation echoes 'Ode to the West Wind'. But the prose-passage's resolute linguistic energy and its implicit faith that real action can be created by contemplating words of action – the verbs to 'love, and admire, and trust, and hope, and endure' – even more obviously guide us as to how we should read the very poem that this prose introduces. That poem ends, insisting that the mind which 'creates' is the one that 'contemplates'. We can learn 'To love', 'to bear', and above all, 'to hope' through studying the tale of a mythical 'Titan' like Prometheus and familiarizing our minds with its images of human 'glory'.

According to Aeschylus, Prometheus had himself invented 'the combining of letters' which is 'the creative Mother of the Muses' art' (*Prometheus Bound*, Act I, line 257). He was thus the first poet; and all true 'Poets', according to Shelley in 'A Defense of Poetry', 'are not only the authors of language . . . they are the institutors of laws, and the founders of civil society and the inventors of the arts of life'. From a writer who so often felt impotent before the brutal legislation of the society into which he had been born, this may sound an absurd claim. Yet perhaps this grandiose generalization, like so much in Shelley's writing, uses the continuing present to evoke precisely those past achievements and future possibilities that present-day events made least credible. His most defiantly optimistic writing is not a retreat from, but a response to, that modern, highly *un*civil society where renegade poets like Wordsworth now slavishly supported laws that had been made by the servants of Jupiter rather than the heirs of Prometheus.

The true role of literature, which could only be misrepresented by too localized a focus on those contemporary specifics, had been proved earlier when England was being drawn towards its own revolution. Shelley argues, in 'A Philosophical View of Reform' that 'Shakespeare and Lord Bacon and the great writers of the age of

Elizabeth and James the 1st' had indeed, however indirectly, insti-
tuted laws and founded a more civil society. They had developed 'a
new spirit in men's minds' which led to the trial of Charles I. There
'one of those chiefs of a conspiracy whose impunity has been the
consecration of crime' was finally brought 'to public justice'.

The Preface to *Prometheus Unbound* returns to this moment in
which English democrats nerved themselves to kill a king and to
dismantle the established church. Milton, that 'Republican . . . and
bold enquirer into morals and religion', typifies that 'golden age of
our literature which shook to dust the oldest and most oppressive
form of the Christian Religion' (Webb, p. 31). But Milton wrote his
greatest poem, whose rebel-hero Satan is 'the only imaginary being
resembling in any degree Prometheus' (Webb, p. 30), after the
counter-revolutionary forces of Crown and Church had regained
their stranglehold. His optimisms too had to survive times in which
high claims for the power of libertarian poetry seemed merely
fanciful. Yet, in hindsight, Milton's achievement makes it reasonable, even in the dark days of 1819, to regard literature as a massive,
if invisible, force:

> The great writers of our own age are, we have reason to suppose, the
> fore-runners of some unimagined change in our social condition or the
> opinions which cement it. The cloud of mind is discharging its
> collected lightning. . .   (Webb, p. 31)

Literature's 'golden age' is not just a fading memory. It represents a
basic force which will re-emerge to transform the future.

However, according to another passage of prose written in
August 1819, at much the same time as the Preface:

> The change should commence among the higher orders, or anarchy
> will only be the last flash before despotism.[13]

The fiery explosion of the people-monster, Shelley sometimes feared,
might change nothing if there were not already enough changed
minds amongst the intellectuals:

> Had there been more of those men, France would not now be a beacon
> to warn us of the hazard and horror of Revolutions, but a pattern for
> society . . . an example for the gradual and peaceful regeneration of
> the world.[14]

Shelley's ambivalence in handling 'the master theme of the epoch in
which we live – the French Revolution',[15] inevitably makes interpretation of *Prometheus Unbound* difficult.

Yet such difficulty seems to me integral to the thoughtfulness
which underpins the poetry's verbal music and makes the work such
a remarkable achievement. Shelley, like Wordsworth and Blake, here
attempts a major epic, in emulation of Milton. Shelley's response,
both to the Miltonic example's sheer scale and to the localized

demands of his own age, seems more boldly direct than that achieved by either of his rivals. Written while he was aged only 26–7, the poem is for me an extraordinary demonstration of that proper self-confidence which all its richly orchestrated voices are designed to recommend.

7. Conclusion

I have tried to emphasize the politics – in however broad a definition of that term – that seem to me the central subject of Shelley's verse. I have also concentrated, when discussing the stance adopted within each poem, on self-esteem and optimism – however strenuously achieved and precariously retained – as the attitudes that the poet tends to adopt himself, and to recommend to the reader.

But limits of space prevent my now moving on to offer detailed discussion of Shelley's last poems; and these strike some readers as being different in both subject and stance. The political element supposedly becomes more peripheral and the poet's own personal situation more central. The stance is argued to be increasingly one of self-doubt, or even of despair.

This is not my own view. I believe that, even in the earlier verse, Shelley's sophisticated account of politics is already so wide-ranging that it often foregrounds his own experience as a private citizen or explores his own obligations as a public poet. I also believe that the optimism for which so much of that verse struggles is frequently defined by evocation of an opposite frame of mind. It seems to me that the temptations of despondency and cynicism, the then fashionable attitudes that recent European history seemed to validate, are on the poetry's agenda from the outset.

Conversely, I read many of Shelley's last poems as still striving to discover hope even in those apparently forlorn situations that they do characteristically explore; and some of the later poetry still seems to me recognisably political verse, even if one uses that phrase in a relatively narrow sense.

To form your own opinion on whether, towards the end of

Shelley's writing career, there is a significant shift, try the following sequence.

Read first the two choruses from *Hellas* (Webb pp. 158–9). Both do certainly open with assertions of a more obvious optimism than is displayed in their closing lines; but should we see the conclusions as replacing attitudes that are now to be seen as discredited; or merely as adding, to a still standing promise about future potential, a balancing acknowledgement of recent set-backs? Does each poem simply turn away from jauntily asserted hope to a despair just as glib? Or does it instead complicate its definition of hope, expanding it to embrace the kind of warning without which we might have dismissed the initial claim of the opening lines as merely naive?

You must decide how far your own reading of these lyrics should take account of the fact that both were designed to be sung by particular characters in a play's specific plot-situation (See Webb's notes, pp. 223–4). And you should be prepared to notice potential ambiguities in songs whose straightforward vocabulary may be stirred by syntax into telling equivocations. Look, for instance, at the second lyric's closing stanza. That poses the 'return' of 'hate and death' explicitly as a question, not an asserted certainty. It does then move out of its interrogative grammar to state firmly that 'The world *is* weary of the past'. But does the next line refer despairingly to 'The world' or merely to the embittering memory of the recent 'past', when praying 'O might it die or rest at last!'?

Then explore the lyrics to Jane Williams that do seem to derive from a painfully specific situation in Shelley's private life. I have to concede that here the poetry is so intimately personal that some biographical information, of the kind that Webb supplies in his notes, is necesssary. One does need to know that the poet was wrestling to control an infatuation that threatened, not only his own relatively long-standing marriage but also that enviably fresher relationship which his close friend, Edward Williams, was still able to enjoy with his young wife. Yet I have already asked you, much earlier in the Guide, to read two of the poems that seem to have been provoked by the guilts and frustrations of this situation. I thought it fair to do so, without inviting you to read one ('When Passion's Trance Is Overpast') as addressed to the poet's helplessly jealous wife; or the other ('One Word Is Too Often Profaned') as aimed at the fascinatingly unavailable wife of the poet's best friend. Both lyrics arguably make sense (perhaps even their best sense) without such a context.

Look at these again, before tackling the more indisputably specific poems. These are 'To Edward Williams' (Webb, p. 164), 'To Jane: The Recollection' (Webb, p. 166), 'To Jane' (Webb, p. 188). Arguably, 'Lines Written in the Bay of Lerici' (Webb, p. 189) belongs here too. Even in these poems, you may find – as I certainly do – many echoes of the earlier verse. You too may decide that these restlessly self-critical poems are not so narrowly obsessed with obligations as husband or friend as to ignore the responsibility of the professional, socially committed poet. Certainly, Shelley's energetic curiosity about the power of words is still implicit throughout these lyrics; and it becomes the explicit subject of some, crucial lines.

The lyrics about Jane were not intended for publication. Indeed, some may have been written on the assumption that they could be kept so secret that they would not be read even by their hypothesized addressees. Their power, in evoking the pain of clandestine feelings, clearly depends on allusions to an intensely private situation; but that intimate allusiveness also allows a proliferation of alternative interpretations which can never be disproved. Disagreement amongst the critics is even more rife in the case of a fragment like the 'Bay of Lerici' lines. These were left unfinished at the time of his death, breaking off, after a penultimate line that is incomplete, in a last line whose wording is a matter for dispute by textual editors. Not knowing how many more lines Shelley had intended to add, let alone in what direction they might have carried the poem, critics are unusually free to guess at the work's overall import.

The same problem arises with what, in spite of its similarly unfinished manuscript, is increasingly acknowledged as the most powerful of Shelley's last poems, and argued by some to be one of the greatest works he ever wrote: 'The Triumph of Life' (Webb, p. 171). Here the references to recent European history and the central role given to Rousseau, the father of the French Revolution, prevent any reader arguing that the poetry has forgotten politics. Nevertheless, the equivocal title in which 'Triumph' may be a pun and the shadowy symbolism established by the narrative's dream framework compound the indecisiveness of the text's breaking off far short of its intended conclusion. They leave the poem open to an extraordinary variety of interpretations. It has even been argued that here Shelley summons up the ghost of his past political commitment only to reject it as a futile fantasy that cannot make the facts of mortality and human helplessness less bitter. To me, 'The Triumph of Life' seems the last and perhaps the most sturdy of a long line of poems in which Shelley presses his own optimism against the bitterest actualities, testing it to the very brink of destruction; but only to render it a weapon that intelligent grown-ups can no longer patronize.

This poem was virtually ignored for over a century until T. S. Eliot singled it out for praise.[1] Numerous articles on the poem were followed by a complete book in 1965[2] and in 1979; when five of the most daring of post-structuralist critics collaborated to produce *Deconstruction and Criticism*, no less than three of them chose to make 'The Triumph of Life' their key-text.[3]

Though Shelley's reputation did briefly stabilize at a low ebb after F. R. Leavis' attack in 1936,[4] the overall history is not a simple matter of Shelley's oeuvre moving as a body down or up the league-table. Quite different poems have been cited at one time or another as typifying what matters most in Shelley. Moreover, even when faced by the same poem, readers have been able to differ widely as to which aspects deserved praise. It was, for instance, the more lyrical passages of *Queen Mab* that struck an 1821 reviewer as 'brilliant' and 'noble'. These were to be enjoyed best by ignoring as far as possible the poem's revolutionary ideas. The latter constituted a 'hideous blasphemy' that could only leave the reader experiencing a 'mixture of sorrow, indignation and loathing'.[5] Yet, it was these very ideas that, in the late 1840s and early 1850s would make the poem famous as 'the Chartist's Bible'; and would, by the end of the century lead George Bernard Shaw and other Fabians to carry copies of Shelley in their pockets.[6]

At present, a renewed interest in those ideas is one of the reasons that Shelley's writings are now the subject of greater curiosity and respect than they have ever enjoyed before. That interest initiated much of the textual scholarship which is finally allowing us to know, for the first time, precisely what Shelley did write. But there is another, distinguishable if closely related, strand to the current enthusiasm. That is our growing appreciation of Shelley's verbal craftsmanship.

The brief period in which it was fashionable to see Shelley as both a sloppy thinker and a careless writer is over. The consensus has swung back to a directly opposite position: to where, amongst Shelley's fellow-professionals, it had always tended to be. Wordsworth called him 'one of the best artists of us all: I mean in workmanship of style'.[7] Tennyson honoured Shelley's skill by frequent close imitation.[8] Browning, as early as 1833, celebrated Shelley as a mentor in *Pauline* (lines 151–229); and was a founding member in 1886 of the Shelley Society.[9] Shelley's influence on Thomas Hardy's poetry has only recently begun to be appreciated.[10]

But it is Yeats who is perhaps the greatest of Shelley's imitators.[11] If you still doubt that Shelley's poems are, at the very least, worth arguing with, you could investigate some of the reverently combative ripostes that Yeats offers to specific passages of Shelley's verse. Compare lines 5–8 of Yeats' 'Second Coming' with their inspiration in Act I lines 625–7 of *Prometheus Unbound* (a poem which Yeats heard read aloud as a child until it became his 'sacred book');[12] or lines 9–12 of Yeats' 'Two Songs from a Play' with their original in the third stanza of the second Chorus from *Hellas*.

Yeats, like so many who admire Shelley in youth, later grew dissatisfied with the verse as he grew further out of sympathy with its politics. After Ireland's Easter Rising and other examples of the 'terrible beauty' that political commitment can create, it was Shelley's work that Yeats blamed for 'the tumultuous . . . tragic lives' that he had seen so many 'friends or acquaintances' endure: 'I attributed to his direct or indirect influence their Jacobin frenzies'. Such phrasing seems to collapse the century that had passed since Pitt's Tories feared a French-style revolution in Britain. Shelley, who had himself tried to rouse a rebellion in Dublin and yet hoped to free Ireland without bloodshed, might or might not have taken Yeats' accusation as a compliment.

But Shelley would surely have been pleased at Yeats' more youthful enthusiasm which the same essay recalls:

> When I was in my early twenties Shelley was much talked about . . . He had shared our curiosities, our political problems, our conviction that despite all experience to the contrary, love is enough.[13]

For those sorts of reasons, and for the unfailingly vigorous and subtle language which first drew the young Yeats towards the poem's passionate ideas, Shelley is once again being much talked about. It seems to me a topic that can only do good.

Notes

Abbreviations:
Holmes – Richard Holmes, *Shelley: The Pursuit*, Quartet Books 1976.
Letters – *The Letters of Percy Bysshe Shelley*, edited by Frederick L. Jones (2 volumes), Clarenden Press 1964.
Works – *The Complete Works of Percy Bysshe Shelley* edited by Roger Ingpen and Walter E. Peck (10 volumes), Ernest Benn (London), Gordian Press (New York), 1965.

Chapter 1
1 Arnold's review of Edward Dowden's *Life of Percy Bysshe Shelley* (*The Nineteenth Century*, January 1888), reprinted as 'Shelley' in Arnold's *Essays in Criticism* (Second Series 1888, reprinted 1908) p. 244, pp. 251–2.

2 'Shelley', *op. cit.*: concluding sentences. Earlier, the essay has jeered at Shelley's politics, his 'nonsense about tyrants and priests'.
3 *Letters*, Vol. II, No. 660, p. 344.

Chapter 2

1 William Wordsworth, 'Preface' to 1802 edition of *Lyrical Ballads*.
2 *The Revolt of Islam:* Canto II, stanza xliii, line 1045; *The Complete Poetical Works of Percy Bysshe Shelley*, edited by Thomas Hutchinson, Oxford University Press 1905, p. 63.
3 'Ode to the West Wind', line 69: Webb, p. 78.
4 Fox, the leader of the Whigs in the British Parliament, described the Revolution as 'the greatest event that ever happened for the happiness of mankind'. See Colin Brooks, 'England 1782–1832: the historical context', p. 40 in *The Romantics* edited by Stephen Prickett, Methuen 1981.
5 *The Prelude*, Book X, lines 691–693 in the version written in 1805, but not published until after Wordsworth's death in 1850.
6 'Apology for the French Revolution' (not published in Wordsworth's lifetime), *The Prose Works of William Wordsworth*, ed. A. B. Grosart, 1876, Vol. I, pp. 3–5.
7 Southey and Coleridge, *The Fall of Robespierre*, Act II, lines 263–7, quoted Kenneth Curry, *Southey*, Routledge & Kegan Paul, 1975.
8 *New Letters of Robert Southey*, ed. Kenneth Curry, New York 1965, Vol. I, p. 81.
9 *Coleridge's Poetical Works*, edited by E. H. Coleridge, Oxford University Press 1912, p. 244.
10 Holmes, p. 94.
11 *Letters*, Vol. I, No. 160, p. 231.
12 Brooks, *op. cit.*, p. 58.
13 Holmes, p. 10.
14 Holmes, p. 95.
15 Holmes, p. 10.
16 Leigh Hunt, *Lord Byron and his Contemporaries*, 1828, Vol. I, pp. 300–5.
17 *Letters*, Vol. I, no. 49, p. 55.
18 *Letters*, Vol. I, no. 168, p. 256.
19 *Letters*, Vol. I, no. 172, p. 263.
20 *Works*, Vol. V, pp. 263–4.
21 Holmes, p. 102.
22 *Letters*, Vol. I, no. 179, p. 260, note 8; no. 173; p. 269, note 6.
23 'Dedication' to *Laon and Cythna*, later *The Revolt of Islam*, stanza 13, Hutchinson, p. 40.
24 See Holmes, pp. 43 and 51–4; and Paul Foot, *Red Shelley*, Sidgwick & Jackson 1980, pp. 27 and 34.
25 *Letters*, Vol. I, no. 49, p. 54.
26 Paul Foot, *Red Shelley*, Sidgwick & Jackson 1980, p. 28.
27 Pamela Horn, *Life and Labour in Rural England 1760–1850*, Macmillan 1987, p. 54.
28 *Letters*, Vol. I, no. 155, p. 213; (December 26, 1811).
29 Byron, *Childe Harolde* Canto III, line 154 (stanza 18).
30 It was during Shelley's life-time that the word 'radical' emerged with its

current meaning: perhaps helped by this image which had been used also by Tom Paine: 'Lay then the axe to the root, and teach governments humanity. It is their sanguinary punishments which corrupt mankind', *The Rights of Man*, p. 33.

31 E. P. Thompson, *The Making of the English Working Class*, Victor Gollancz Ltd, 1965, p. 713.

32 *Ibid.*

33 *Letters*, Vol. II, no. 633, pp. 300–1; no. 662, p. 350; and no. 664, p. 356.

34 *Letters*, Vol. I, no. 148, p. 202; no. 155, p. 214.

Chapter 3

1 D. H. Reiman and S. B. Powers, *Shelley's Poetry and Prose*, W. W. Norton and Company 1977, p. 94.

2 A. D. M. Hughes, *The Nascent Mind of Shelley*, Oxford University Press 1947, p. 42, note 1.

3 *The Oxford Anthology of English Literature: Romantic Poetry and Prose*, edited by Harold Bloom and Lionel Trilling, Oxford University Press 1973, p. 408.

4 Desmond King-Hele, *Shelley His Thought and Work*, Macmillan 1960, p. 69.

5 *A Vindication of the Rights of Woman* [1792], edited by Miriam Brody Krammick, Pelican Books 1975, p. 134.

6 'A Discourse on the Manners of the Ancients: Relative to the Subject of Love', *Works*, Vol. VII, p. 228.

7 '"The Banquet" Translated from Plato', *Works*, Vol. VII, p. 206.

8 K. N. Cameron, *Percy Bysshe Shelley: Selected Poetry and Prose*, p. 515.

9 'Essay on Christianity', *Works* Vol. VI, p. 231.

10 *Queen Mab*, Note to VIII lines 203–207: *The Complete Poetical Works of Percy Bysshe Shelley*, edited by Thomas Hutchinson, Oxford University Press, p. 825.

11 'A Defence of Poetry', *Works*, Vol. VII, p. 140.

12 'Essay on Christianity', *Works*, Vol. VI, p. 245.

13 'A Defence of Poetry', *Works*, Vol. VII, p. 136.

14 See Patricia Hodgart, *A Preface to Shelley*, Longman 1985, p. 146; and Angela Leighton, *Shelley and the Sublime*, Cambridge University Press 1984, p. 12 ff.

15 *Works*, Vol. VI, p. 195.

Chapter 4

1 Byron, *Childe Harolde*, Canto 4, stanzas cxxii–cxxiii.

2 You might look back, for instance, at 'Mont Blanc', lines 18–19, 67, 87–8, 104–7, 118–19, 137–8; or 'The Cloud', lines 8–12. Explore too 'Ode to Liberty' (Webb, p. 91) and 'Goethe's Faust' (Webb, p. 169), lines 17–24.

3 Reiman and Powers, *Shelley's Poetry and Prose*, p. 379, note 7.

4 T. Webb, *Shelley: A Voice Not Understood*, Manchester University Press 1977, p. 41.

5 Reiman and Powers, *Shelley's Poetry and Prose*, p. 103, notes 7 and 8.

Chapter 5

1 E. P. Thompson, *op. cit.*, p. 681.
2 *The Autobiography of Samuel Bamford*, Vol. 2: *Passages in the Life of a Radical*, edited by W. H. Chaloner, Frank Cass & Co. Ltd, 1967, pp. 179–80.

Chapter 6

1 'On Life', *Works*, Vol. VI, p. 196.
2 'A Philosophical View of Reform', *Works*, Vol. VII, pp. 53–4.
3 See R. J. White, *Waterloo to Peterloo*, Heinemann 1957, p. 174; and, for Shelley's interest in the trial, his 'An Address to the People . . .' (*Works*, Vol. VI, pp. 71–82).
4 'Speculations on Morals', *Works*, Vol. VII, p. 74.
5 Shelley was familiar with a number of works by the celebrated orientalist, Sir William Jones; and works by other enthusiasts such as *Hindu Pantheon* (1810) by Edward Moor.
6 *Works*, Vol. VII, pp. 53–4.
7 Paul Dawson, *The Unacknowledged Legislator*, Oxford University Press, 1980, pp. 116–17.
8 Paul Foot, *Red Shelley*, Sidgwick & Jackson 1980, pp. 198–9.
9 *Queen Mab*, VI, lines 216–19.
10 Preface to *Hellas*.
11 See the note to Act I, line 371 in Webb, p. 198.
12 Angela Leighton, *Shelley and the Sublime*, Cambridge University Press 1984, pp. 91–2.
13 *Letters*, Vol. II, no. 511, p. 115.
14 'Proposals for an Association', *Works*, Vol. V, p. 265.
15 *Letters*, Vol. I, No. 361, p. 504.

Chapter 7

1 T. S. Eliot, *The Use of Poetry and the Use of Criticism* (1933), p. 90.
2 Donald H. Reiman, *Shelley's 'The Triumph of Life': A Critical Study*, Illinois Studies in Language and Literature 55 (1965).
3 See Paul de Man, 'Shelley Disfigured', Jacques Derrida, 'Living on. Border lines' and J. Hillis Miller, 'The Critic as Host' in Harold Bloom *et al.*, *Deconstruction and Criticism*, Routledge & Kegan Paul, 1979.
4 F. R. Leavis, *Revaluation* (London, 1936), pp. 203–32.
5 Unsigned review, *The Literary Gazette and Journal of Belles Lettres* (19 May 1821) no. 226, 305–8. See James E. Barcus (ed.), *Shelley: The Critical Heritage* (Routledge & Kegan Paul 1975), pp. 74–80.
6 Kenneth Muir, 'Shelley's Heirs', *Penguin New Writing* no. 26 (1946), p. 117 and p. 132.
7 A judgment made in 1827. Quoted Newman Ivey White, *Shelley*, Alfred A. Knopf, 1940, II p. 637, citing Christopher Wordsworth, *Memoirs of William Wordsworth* (1851) II p. 474.
8 Christopher Ricks in his edition of *The Poems of Tennyson* (Longmans 1987) traces about fifty echoes in poetry written up to and including the 1850s.

9 For other famous names amongst the Society's four hundred members, see Newman Ivy White, *Shelley* (1940), II p. 412.

10 See Phylis Bartlett's essays in *Publications of Modern Language Association* LXX (September 1955), pp. 624–35 and in *Keats–Shelley Journal* IV (Winter 1955), pp. 15–29.

11 See Miriam Allott, 'Attitudes to Shelley: the vagaries of a critical reputation' in *Essays on Shelley*, ed. Miriam Allott, Liverpool University Press 1982, pp. 27–9.

12 W. B. Yeats, *Autobiographies* (London 1955), p. 11. 'The Philosophy of Shelley's Poetry' (1900), reprinted in *Essays and Introductions* (London 1961).

13 W. B. Yeats, 'Prometheus Unbound', *The Spectator*, CL (17 March 1935), p. 367.

Suggestions for Further Reading

Works by Shelley

At the time this Guide is being completed, there is still no satisfactory edition of the complete poems, though one is in preparation. Edited by G. M. Matthews and Kelvin Everest, it will be published by Longmans and undoubtedly become the authoritative text. The first of its three volumes which will cover the earlier verse up to 1816 is scheduled for publication in 1989.

Meanwhile, the least unsatisfactory alternatives are the Oxford edition edited by Thomas Hutchinson in 1904 (revised by G. M. Matthews in 1970); C. D. Locock's usefully annotated edition of the complete poems (Methuen 1911); Peter Butter's edition of *Alastor, Prometheus Unbound, Adonais and other Poems* (Collins 1970); and *The Complete Works of Percy Bysshe Shelley*, 10 volumes, edited by Roger Ingpen and Walter E. Peck (Ernest Benn 1965).

This last can be used also for the prose; but, for that, a less bulky and expensive alternative is *Shelley's Prose or The Trumpet of a Prophecy*, edited by David Lee Clark. This was published by the University of New Mexico Press in 1954 but use the corrected edition of 1966. Even this still contains a

number of annotations that other Shelley scholars see as eccentric, particularly as to dates of composition. However, Clark includes all the prose
except the letters and the two novels. For these consult *The Letters of Percy
Bysshe Shelley*, edited by Frederick L. Jones; and the World's Classics
edition of *Zastrozzi* and *St. Irvyne*, edited by Stephen C. Behrendt (Oxford
University Press 1986).

Useful selections that include both verse and prose are *Percy Bysshe
Shelley: Selected Poetry and Prose*, edited by K. N. Cameron (Holt Rinehart
and Winston 1964); *Shelley's Poetry and Prose*, edited by Donald H.
Reiman and Sharon B. Powers (W. W. Norton 1977); and (perhaps best, if
only because of its superb introduction), G. M. Matthews *Selected Poems
and Prose* (Oxford University Press 1964).

Works about Shelley

Biographical

The most recent biography is *Shelley: the Pursuit* by Richard Holmes,
published in 1974 by Wiedenfeld & Nicolson, and re-issued as a reasonably
priced paperback by Quartet Books in 1976. Fuller, if less entertainingly
written, is Newman Ivey White's *Shelley*, 2 vols. (New York 1940). Also
interesting, particularly for the political side of Shelley's life, are two books
by K. N. Cameron: *The Young Shelley: Genesis of a Radical* (Macmillan
1950) and *Shelley: the Golden Years* (Harvard University Press 1974). Some
of Shelley's most important friendships are described in John Buxton's
Byron and Shelley (Macmillan 1968); K. N. Cameron's *Romantic Rebels:
Essays on Shelley and his Circle* (Harvard University Press 1973); and Leigh
Hunt's *Autobiography* (1850). This last should be approached with some
scepticism as should other, but interesting, early works such as T. J. Hogg's
Life of Percy Bysshe Shelley (2 volumes, 1858, Oxford University Press
1906); T. L. Peacock's *Memoirs of Shelley* (1858–1860, Hart-Davis 1970);
and E. J. Trelawney's *Recollections of the Last Days of Shelley and Byron*
(1859).

Critical Works

Lloyd Abbey, *Destroyer and Preserver: Shelley's Skepticism*, University of
    Nebraska Press 1979.
Miriam Allott (ed.), *Essays on Shelley*, Liverpool University Press 1982.
J. E. Barcus (ed.), *Shelley: The Critical Heritage*, Routledge & Kegan Paul
    1975.
Harold Bloom, *Shelley's Mythmaking*, Yale University Press 1959.
Nathaniel Brown, *Sexuality and Feminism in Shelley*, Harvard University
    Press 1979.
Judith Chernaik, *The Lyrics of Shelley*, Case Western Reserve University
    1972.
Richard Cronin, *Shelley's Poetic Thoughts*, Macmillan 1981.
Paul Dawson, *The Unacknowledged Legislator: Shelley and Politics*,
    Oxford University Press, 1983.
Kelvin Everest (ed.), *Shelley Revalued: Essays from the Gregynyog Confer-
    ence*, Leicester University Press, 1983.
Paul Foot, *Red Shelley*, Sidgwick and Jackson 1980.

Carl Grabo, *A Newton Among Poets: Shelley's Use of Science in Prometheus Unbound*, Johns Hopkins Press 1965.
William Keach, *Shelley's Style*, Methuen 1984.
Desmond King-Hele, *Shelley: His Thought and Work* (Macmillan 1960).
Angela Leighton, *Shelley and the Sublime*, Cambridge University Press 1984.
Gerald McNiece, *Shelley and the Revolutionary Idea*, Harvard University Press 1969.
G. M. Matthews, *Shelley*, British Council Pamphlet, Longmans 1970.
D. H. Reiman, *Percy Bysshe Shelley*, Twayne 1976.
Seymour Reiter, *A Study of Shelley's Poetry*, University of New Mexico Press 1967.
George M. Ridenour (ed.), *Shelley: A Collection of Critical Essays*, Prentice-Hall 1965.
Charles E. Robinson, *Shelley and Byron: The Snake and Eagle Wreathed in Fight*, Johns Hopkins University Press 1976.
Patrick Swinden (ed.) *Shelley: Shorter Poems and Lyrics*, Casebook series, Macmillan 1976.
Claire Tomalin, *Shelley and His World*, Thames and Hudson, 1980.
Earl R. Wasserman, *Shelley's Prometheus Unbound: A Critical Reading*, Johns Hopkins Press 1965; and *Shelley: A Critical Reading*, Johns Hopkins Press 1971.
Timothy Webb, *Shelley: A Voice Not Understood*, Manchester University Press 1977; and *The Violet in the Crucible: Shelley and Translation*, Clarenden Press 1976.
Newman Ivey White, *The Unextinguished Hearth: Shelley and his Contemporary Critics* 1938; Octagon Books, 1966.
R. B. Woodings (ed.), *Shelley: Modern Judgements: Selections of Critical Essays*, Macmillan 1968.

Works about the period

A. Aspinall, *Politics and the Press 1780–1850*, Harvester 1973.
Asa Briggs, *The Age of Improvement*, Longmans 1959.
Colin Brooks, 'England 1782–1832: the historical context'. In *The Romantics*, ed. Stephen Prickett, Methuen 1981, pp. 15–76.
Marilyn Butler, *Romantics, Rebels and Reactionaries: English Literature and its Background 1760–1830*, Oxford University Press, 1981.
F. O. Darvall, *Popular Disturbances and Public Order in Regency England*, Oxford University Press, 1934.
Kelvin Everest, 'The Historical Context and the Literary Scene', Units 9–10 of the Open University's course, *Romantic Poetry* (A 362).
Elie Halevy, *England in 1815*, Benn, 1949.
Peter Holt and I. M. Thomis, *Threats of Revolution in Britain 1798–1848*, Macmillan 1977.
Olivia Smith, *The Politics of Language 1791–1819*, Clarenden Press, 1984.
E. P. Thompson, *The Making of the English Working Class*, Victor Gollancz, 1965.
Merryn Williams (ed.), *Revolutions 1775–1830*, Penguin Books, 1971.

Index